Introduction to Representation

Other Books in The Math Process Standards Series

Introduction to Problem Solving: Grades 6–8
(Schackow and O'Connell)
Introduction to Reasoning and Proof: Grades 6–8
(Thompson and Schultz-Ferrell)
Introduction to Communication: Grades 6–8
(O'Connell and Croskey)
Introduction to Connections: Grades 6–8
(Langrall, Meier, Mooney, with Bamberger)

For information on the PreK–2 and 3–5 grades series see the Heinemann website,
www.heinemann.com.

Introduction to Representation
Grades 6–8

Bonnie H. Ennis
Kimberly S. Witeck

The Math Process Standards Series
Susan O'Connell, Series Editor

HEINEMANN
Portsmouth, NH

Heinemann
361 Hanover Street
Portsmouth, NH 03801–3912
www.heinemann.com

Offices and agents throughout the world

The authors and publisher wish to thank those who have generously given permission to reprint borrowed material:

Excerpts from *Principles and Standards for School Mathematics*. Copyright © 2000 by the National Council of Teachers of Mathematics. Reprinted with permission. All rights reserved.

Library of Congress Cataloging-in-Publication Data
Ennis, Bonnie H.
    Introduction to representation : grades 6–8 / Bonnie H. Ennis, Kimberly S. Witeck.
        p. cm. — (Math process standards series)
    Includes bibliographical references.
    ISBN-13: 978-0-325-01387-9
    ISBN-10: 0-325-01387-X
    1. Mathematics—Study and teaching (Middle school).   2. Mathematics—Graphic methods.   3. Mathematical notations   I. Witeck, Kimberly S. II. Title.
    QA11.2.E56 2008
    510.71'2—dc22   2007044376

Editor: Emily Michie Birch
Production coordinator: Elizabeth Valway
Production service: Matrix Productions Inc.
Cover design: Night & Day Design
Cover photography: Joy Bronston Schackow
Composition: Publishers' Design and Production Services, Inc.
CD production: Nicole Russell
Manufacturing: Louise Richardson

Printed in the United States of America on acid-free paper
12   11   10   09   08   ML   1   2   3   4   5

On the CD-ROM

A Guide to the CD-ROM
A Word About the CD Student Activities
Student Activities
   Number and Operations
   Algebra
   Geometry
   Measurement
   Data Analysis and Probability
Representation Toolkit
Representation Across the Content
   Standards Student Activity Pages

In order to be effective mathematicians, students need to develop understanding of critical math content. They need to understand number and operations, algebra, measurement, geometry, and data analysis and probability. Through continued study of these content domains, students gain a comprehensive understanding of mathematics as a subject with varied and interconnected concepts. As math teachers, we attempt to provide students with exposure to, exploration in, and reflection about the many skills and concepts that make up the study of mathematics.

Even with a deep understanding of math content, however, students may lack important skills that can assist them in their development as effective mathematicians. Along with content knowledge, students need an understanding of the processes used by mathematicians. They must learn to problem solve, communicate their ideas, reason through math situations, prove their conjectures, make connections between and among math concepts, and represent their mathematical thinking. Development of content alone does not provide students with the means to explore, express, or apply that content. As we strive to develop effective mathematicians, we are challenged to develop both students' content understanding and process skills.

The National Council of Teachers of Mathematics (2000) has outlined critical content and process standards in its *Principles and Standards for School Mathematics* document. These standards have become the roadmap for the development of textbooks, curriculum materials, and student assessments. These standards have provided a framework for thinking about what needs to be taught in math classrooms and how various skills and concepts can be blended together to create a seamless math curriculum. The first five standards outline content standards and expectations related to number and operations, algebra, geometry, measurement, and data analysis and probability. The second five standards outline the process goals of problem solving, reasoning and proof, communication, connections, and representations. A strong understanding of these standards empowers teachers to identify and select activities within their curricula to produce powerful learning. The standards provide a vision for what teachers hope their students will achieve.

This book is a part of a vital series designed to assist teachers in understanding the NCTM Process Standards and the ways in which they impact and guide student learning. An additional goal of this series is to provide practical ideas to support teachers as they ensure that the acquisition of process skills has a critical place in their math instruction. Through this series, teachers will gain an understanding of each process standard as well as gather ideas for bringing that standard to life within their math classrooms. It offers practical ideas for lesson development, implementation, and assessment that work with any curriculum. Each book in the series focuses on a critical process skill in a highlighted grade band and all books are designed to encourage reflection about teaching and learning. The series also highlights the interconnected nature of the process and content standards by showing correlations between them and showcasing activities that address multiple standards.

Students who develop an understanding of content skills and cultivate the process skills that allow them to apply that content understanding become effective mathematicians. Our goal as teachers is to support and guide students as they develop both their content knowledge and their process skills, so they are able to continue to expand and refine their understanding of mathematics. This series is a guide for math educators who aspire to teach students more than math content. It is a guide to assist teachers in understanding and teaching the critical processes through which students learn and make sense of mathematics.

Susan O'Connell
Series Editor

We would like to thank many people for their support, expertise, guidance, and encouragement during this project. First, thank you to Sue O'Connell for encouraging us to take on this project, for your patient support in reading our work, and for helping to give us a jump-start when we needed it. And to Emily Birch, Executive Editor for Math and Science at Heinemann, thanks for always being available to give feedback, support, and encouragement.

From Bonnie Ennis

To the students, teachers, and administrators of the Wicomico County Public Schools, thank you for your advice, support, and expertise throughout the years. A special thank you to the math professional development coaches of Wicomico County, who continue to amaze me on a daily basis with their creativity, enthusiasm, and willingness to do everything we ask in support of the teachers and students of our district. It is a pleasure to work with such wonderful professionals.

To Sara Chatfield, my thanks for the technology help and to Michele and Kelly thank you for your help in getting work samples. To Mrs. Sullivan's summer school class, your valuable contributions are much appreciated, and to Patty, thank you for being a sounding board; just remember even reading people can do math. The following students were a pleasure to work with and contributed work samples or allowed their photographs to appear in this book: Zachary Bounds, Jenna Harbinson, Taylor Hamilton, Carileigh Jones, Charles Folashade, Ben Bazin, Torres Savage, Ryan Bounds, and Kambria Wright.

From Kimberly Witeck

To the community of teachers and students at Braddock Elementary in Annandale, Virginia, thank you for providing invaluable feedback, support, and your expertise. Thanks especially to Cynthia Botzin, principal at Braddock, for being a model leader for all in the field of education and for allowing me to work with students at the school to gather data and work samples for the book; Judy Hall, Title I math teacher and coach, for her expertise, feedback on particular chapters, and moral support; and Gwenanne Salkind, Title I assistant program supervisor, for her expertise and guidance in clarifying concepts in the book.

Thanks go also to my husband, Chris, my parents, Skip and Jackie Sterling, and my beautiful children, Aidan and Caroline. I love you.

Problem-Solving Standard

Instructional programs from prekindergarten through grade 12 should enable all students to—

- build new mathematical knowledge through problem solving;

- solve problems that arise in mathematics and in other contexts;

- apply and adapt a variety of appropriate strategies to solve problems;

- monitor and reflect on the process of mathematical problem solving.

Reasoning and Proof Standard

Instructional programs from prekindergarten through grade 12 should enable all students to—

- recognize reasoning and proof as fundamental aspects of mathematics;

- make and investigate mathematical conjectures;

- develop and evaluate mathematical arguments and proofs;

- select and use various types of reasoning and methods of proof.

---

* Standards are listed with the permission of the National Council of Teachers of Mathematics (NCTM). NCTM does not endorse the content or validity of these alignments.

Communication Standard

Instructional programs from prekindergarten through grade 12 should enable all students to—

▧ organize and consolidate their mathematical thinking through communication;

▧ communicate their mathematical thinking coherently and clearly to peers, teachers, and others;

▧ analyze and evaluate the mathematical thinking and strategies of others;

▧ use the language of mathematics to express mathematical ideas precisely.

Connections Standard

Instructional programs from prekindergarten through grade 12 should enable all students to—

▧ recognize and use connections among mathematical ideas;

▧ understand how mathematical ideas interconnect and build on one another to produce a coherent whole;

▧ recognize and apply mathematics in contexts outside of mathematics.

Representation Standard

Instructional programs from prekindergarten through grade 12 should enable all students to—

▧ create and use representations to organize, record, and communicate mathematical ideas;

▧ select, apply, and translate among mathematical representations to solve problems;

▧ use representations to model and interpret physical, social, and mathematical phenomena.

NCTM Content Standards and Expectations for Grades 6–8

NUMBER AND OPERATIONS

	Expectations
Instructional programs from prekindergarten through grade 12 should enable all students to—	**In grades 6–8 all students should—**
Understand numbers, ways of representing numbers, relationships among numbers, and number systems	• work flexibly with fractions, decimals, and percents to solve problems; • compare and order fractions, decimals, and percents efficiently and find their approximate locations on a number line; • develop meaning for percents greater than 100 and less than 1; • understand and use ratios and proportions to represent quantitative relationships; • develop an understanding of large numbers and recognize and appropriately use exponential, scientific, and calculator notation; • use factors, multiples, prime factorization, and relatively prime numbers to solve problems; • develop meaning for integers and represent and compare quantities with them.
Understand meanings of operations and how they relate to one another	• understand the meaning and effects of arithmetic operations with fractions, decimals, and integers; • use the associative and commutative properties of addition and multiplication and the distributive property of multiplication over addition to simplify computations with integers, fractions, and decimals; • understand and use the inverse relationships of addition and subtraction, multiplication and division, and squaring and finding square roots to simplify computations and solve problems.

	Expectations
Instructional programs from prekindergarten through grade 12 should enable all students to—	**In grades 6–8 all students should—**
Compute fluently and make reasonable estimates	• select appropriate methods and tools for computing with fractions and decimals from among mental computation, estimation, calculators or computers, and paper and pencil, depending on the situation, and apply the selected methods; • develop and analyze algorithms for computing with fractions, decimals, and integers and develop fluency in their use; • develop and use strategies to estimate the results of rational-number computations and judge the reasonableness of the results; • develop, analyze, and explain methods for solving problems involving proportions, such as scaling and finding equivalent ratios.

ALGEBRA

	Expectations
Instructional programs from prekindergarten through grade 12 should enable all students to—	**In grades 6–8 all students should—**
Understand patterns, relations, and functions	• represent, analyze, and generalize a variety of patterns with tables, graphs, words, and, when possible, symbolic rules; • relate and compare different forms of representation for a relationship; • identify functions as linear or nonlinear and contrast their properties from tables, graphs, or equations.
Represent and analyze mathematical situations and structures using algebraic symbols	• develop an initial conceptual understanding of different uses of variables;

	Expectations
Instructional programs from prekindergarten through grade 12 should enable all students to—	**In grades 6–8 all students should—**
	• explore relationships between symbolic expressions and graphs of lines, paying particular attention to the meaning of intercept and slope; • use symbolic algebra to represent situations and to solve problems, especially those that involve linear relationships; • recognize and generate equivalent forms for simple algebraic expressions and solve linear equations.
Use mathematical models to represent and understand quantitative relationships	• model and solve contextualized problems using various representations, such as graphs, tables, and equations.
Analyze change in various contexts	• use graphs to analyze the nature of changes in quantities in linear relationships.

GEOMETRY

	Expectations
Instructional programs from prekindergarten through grade 12 should enable all students to—	**In grades 6–8 all students should—**
Analyze characteristics and properties of two- and three-dimensional geometric shapes and develop mathematical arguments about geometric relationships	• precisely describe, classify, and understand relationships among types of two- and three-dimensional objects using their defining properties; • understand relationships among the angles, side lengths, perimeters, areas, and volumes of similar objects; • create and critique inductive and deductive arguments concerning geometric ideas and relationships, such as congruence, similarity, and the Pythagorean relationship.

	Expectations
Instructional programs from prekindergarten through grade 12 should enable all students to—	**In grades 6–8 all students should—**
Specify locations and describe spatial relationships using coordinate geometry and other representational systems	• use coordinate geometry to represent and examine the properties of geometric shapes; • use coordinate geometry to examine special geometric shapes, such as regular polygons or those with pairs of parallel or perpendicular sides.
Apply transformations and use symmetry to analyze mathematical situations	• describe sizes, positions, and orientations of shapes under informal transformations such as flips, turns, slides, and scaling; • examine the congruence, similarity, and line or rotational symmetry of objects using transformations.
Use visualization, spatial reasoning, and geometric modeling to solve problems	• draw geometric objects with specified properties, such as side lengths or angle measures; • use two-dimensional representations of three-dimensional objects to visualize and solve problems such as those involving surface area and volume; • use visual tools such as networks to represent and solve problems; • use geometric models to represent and explain numerical and algebraic relationships; • recognize and apply geometric ideas and relationships in areas outside the mathematics classroom, such as art, science, and everyday life.

MEASUREMENT

	Expectations
Instructional programs from prekindergarten through grade 12 should enable all students to—	**In grades 6–8 all students should—**
Understand measurable attributes of objects and the units, systems, and processes of measurement	• understand both metric and customary systems of measurement; • understand relationships among units and convert from one unit to another within the same system; • understand, select, and use units of appropriate size and type to measure angles, perimeter, area, surface area, and volume.
Apply appropriate techniques, tools, and formulas to determine measurements	• use common benchmarks to select appropriate methods for estimating measurements; • select and apply techniques and tools to accurately find length, area, volume, and angle measures to appropriate levels of precision; • develop and use formulas to determine the circumference of circles and the area of triangles, parallelograms, trapezoids, and circles and develop strategies to find the area of more-complex shapes; • develop strategies to determine the surface area and volume of selected prisms, pyramids, and cylinders; • solve problems involving scale factors, using ratio and proportion; • solve simple problems involving rates and derived measurements for such attributes as velocity and density.

Instructional programs from prekindergarten through grade 12 should enable all students to—	Expectations
	In grades 6–8 all students should—
Formulate questions that can be addressed with data and collect, organize, and display relevant data to answer them	• formulate questions, design studies, and collect data about a characteristic shared by two populations or different characteristics within one population;
	• select, create, and use appropriate graphical representations of data, including histograms, box plots, and scatterplots.
Select and use appropriate statistical methods to analyze data	• find, use, and interpret measures of center and spread, including mean and interquartile range;
	• discuss and understand the correspondence between data sets and their graphical representations, especially histograms, stem-and-leaf plots, box plots, and scatterplots.
Develop and evaluate inferences and predictions that are based on data	• use observations about differences between two or more samples to make conjectures about the populations from which the samples were taken;
	• make conjectures about possible relationships between two characteristics of a sample on the basis of scatterplots of the data and approximate lines of fit;
	• use conjectures to formulate new questions and plan new studies to answer them.
Understand and apply basic concepts of probability	• understand and use appropriate terminology to describe complementary and mutually exclusive events;
	• use proportionality and a basic understanding of probability to make and test conjectures about the results of experiments and simulations;
	• compute probabilities for simple compound events, using such methods as organized lists, tree diagrams, and area models.

Introduction to Representations

The Representation Standard

The ways in which mathematical ideas are represented is fundamental to how people can understand and use those ideas.

—National Council of Teachers of Mathematics,
Principles and Standards for School Mathematics

What Are Representations?

What do we mean when we ask students to show their work? Are we asking them to show the numeric computations and steps they took in reaching a solution to a division problem? Are we looking for the right steps in solving an equation? Are we asking them to somehow put on paper the processes and thinking they went through as they developed a solution to a multi-step problem that involves fractions? What does it truly mean to ask students to represent their mathematical thinking, and how can we support, model for, and encourage students to put on paper their interpretations of the mathematical models that helped them make those crucial connections between the concrete and the abstract? Representing their solutions is one of the means by which students can communicate to others their mathematical thinking and at the same time clarify in their own mind what meaning lies in the mathematics. Although manipulatives provide students with an opportunity to model the mathematics at hand, they are just that: models. It is up to the teacher to help students make the connections between the models, the mathematics, and the real-world applications. Only by making these connections will students truly understand and internalize the concepts of math. Once that connection has been made, students can represent their thinking in words, pictures or symbols, and diagrams and apply their knowledge to more complex problem-solving situations.

Representations take many forms: an algorithm that represents a problem situation, a four-quadrant graph that represents data collected in the classroom, a model that shows the relationship between a fraction and a percentage, or a diagram that illustrates area or perimeter. Numbers, pictures, diagrams, equations, graphs, and models are all forms of mathematical representations. In the past, teachers may have chosen to introduce a concept by teaching the standard algorithm from the start, but research is now supporting the practice of providing multiple opportunities for students to construct meanings while developing representations of their understandings. Those representations are valuable tools through which students can not only explore more complex ideas but also enhance their mathematical thinking.

The National Council of Teachers of Mathematics' *Principles and Standards for School Mathematics* (2000) describes representations as fundamental to understanding and applying mathematics, and it makes three recommendations for using them in the mathematics classroom:

1. teachers should employ "representations to model and interpret physical, social, and mathematical phenomena" (NCTM 2000, 70);

2. students should be familiar with and comprehend various representations that can be used to describe phenomena; and

3. students should use mathematical representations to organize their thinking and reflect on numerical or geometric information.

Representations, instead of being taught to students, are valuable ways in which students can explore their own math thinking. Finding ways to represent their ideas pushes students to think more deeply about those ideas as they determine ways to communicate them to others. Providing students with a way of working through their thought processes, representations give us insight into our students' understandings. When students use base ten blocks to model multiplication problems, draw a scaled diagram, and create a stem-and-leaf plot to organize and analyze data, they are using various forms of representation to demonstrate their mathematical thinking. It is important that we give students many opportunities to represent their thinking and guide them to become proficient in representation. As they become more comfortable creating representations of their ideas, their mathematical thinking will greatly expand, as will their ability to communicate about that thinking.

Representation is both a process and a product by which students are able to explore and sort out mathematical concepts as well as communicate mathematically with their peers. Because representation is both a process and a product, students need many and varied opportunities to explore and sort mathematical concepts and to communicate these concepts to their peers. They need opportunities that will ultimately guide them toward more conventional forms of representation, facilitating their mathematical thinking and deepening their understanding. By enabling students to use a wide variety of representations, we are helping them to assemble a repertoire of tools from which to draw when exploring mathematical concepts.

What Is the Representation Standard?

Principles and Standards for School Mathematics (NCTM 2000) has outlined standards for both math content and math processes. The content standards help us identify key math content that is critical to students' understanding of mathematics, and the process standards help us identify those processes through which students learn and apply math content. Representation is a critical math process that supports students in their learning of math and their ability to express that learning.

In NCTM's original standards document, *Curriculum and Evaluation Standards for School Mathematics* (1989), representation was included as a part of the communication standard, one of the four process standards in the original document. In the 2000 document, five process standards are outlined, with communication and representation individually addressed. NCTM now treats representation as its own process standard to address the broad scope of representation and its importance in learning mathematics. It has been recognized that the ability to represent ideas is fundamental to the study of mathematics.

In *Principles and Standards for School Mathematics*, NCTM recommends that instructional programs from prekindergarten through grade 12 should enable all students to

- create and use representations to organize, record, and communicate mathematical ideas;

- select, apply, and translate among mathematical representations to solve problems; and

- use representations to model and interpret physical, social, and mathematical phenomena.

The abilities to create representations to illustrate ideas, communicate thinking through representations, determine which representation would best fit a concept or idea, and use representation to model math situations are all critical components of this standard.

How Can Representation Support Student Learning?

Representation is both about helping students find their own ways to represent math ideas and about helping them understand conventional representations of math ideas (e.g., fractions, decimals, ratios, expanded notation, charts, graphs, diagrams). Students should be encouraged to represent their ideas in ways that make sense to them. Seeing a variety of student-created representations can help teachers recognize where there may be hidden misconceptions, but it helps reveal the level of proficiency a student has with a concept or process. In Taylor's work, we can clearly see that not only is he able to correctly identify the possible outcomes, but he has also shown that he can apply that knowledge to new and different situations. His explanation adds information for the teacher about his understanding of possible outcomes.

Although many representations are conventional, not all students will show their thinking in conventional ways. It is important that we allow them to work through their thinking in ways that make sense to them and then guide them toward more conventional representations to assist them in better understanding mathematics as well as to enable others to understand their thought processes.

In this book, you will see many examples of ways you can provide students with opportunities to represent their thinking and of how to enable them to use those representations in meaningful ways. The process of representation, which is the act of putting one's ideas into words, pictures, numbers, or symbols, is as important as the product: the actual representation of those ideas. We must provide students with many opportunities and ongoing support as they attempt to represent their own ideas and as they explore standard ways to represent math ideas.

In addition to providing students with many opportunities to represent their thinking, we must expose them to a variety of representations. When teaching the concept

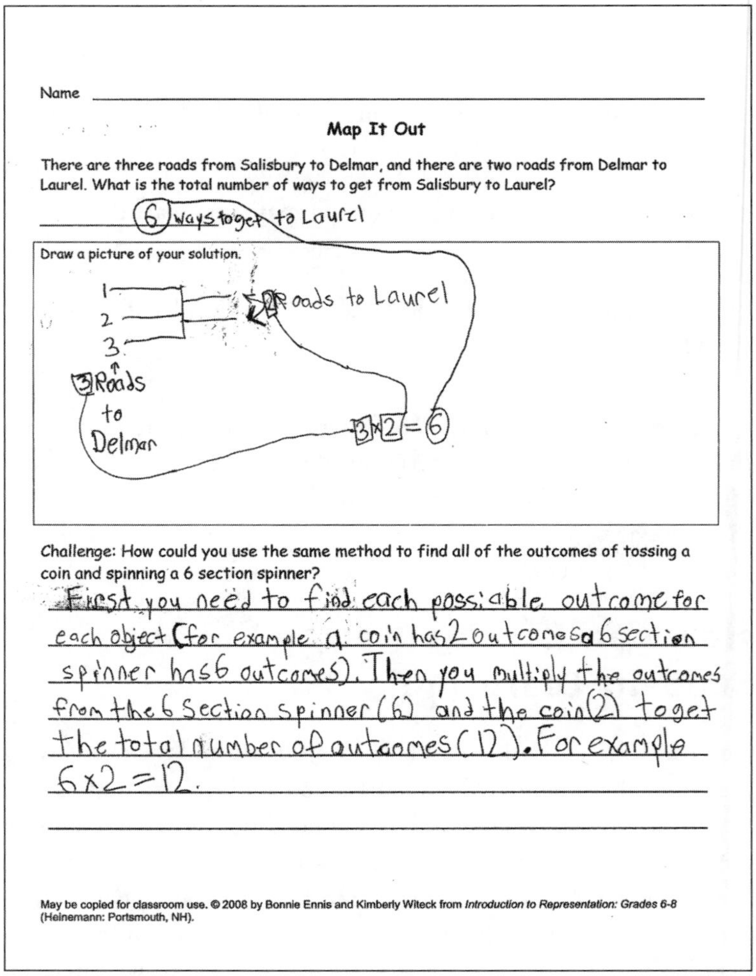

Name

Map It Out

There are three roads from Salisbury to Delmar, and there are two roads from Delmar to Laurel. What is the total number of ways to get from Salisbury to Laurel?

6 ways to get to Laurel

Draw a picture of your solution.

Challenge: How could you use the same method to find all of the outcomes of tossing a coin and spinning a 6 section spinner?

First you need to find each possiable outcome for each object (for example a coin has 2 outcomes a 6 section spinner has 6 outcomes). Then you multiply the outcomes from the 6 section spinner (6) and the coin (2) to get the total number of outcomes (12). For example 6x2=12.

Figure I–1 *Taylor's work with possible outcomes*

of division as fair share, a teacher may chose to provide students with concrete objects such as base ten blocks and counters that they could manipulate to illustrate equal groups. It is important, too, to include in our instruction other ways of representing division, such as through pictures, numbers, and words. In addition, as students' mathematical thinking matures, they learn to choose more appropriate ways of representing their ideas and information. For example, a sixth-grade student, when faced with a set of data, might need to decide which graphic representation would be most appropriate for organizing and then analyzing the data, whether it is a bar graph, a stem-and-leaf plot, a line graph, or a box-and-whiskers plot. A seventh-grade student being asked to demonstrate understanding of the difference between volume and area may choose to use the same shape in his or her representation but identify the different concepts through the appropriate algorithms. By encouraging students to use multiple representations, we help them build a repertoire from which to choose strategies for solving mathematical problems.

Finally, students should use representations to model real-world phenomena. An eighth-grade student might record the ups and downs of a particular stock from the daily stock market report for a month and then represent the data on a line graph to effectively analyze it. A sixth-grade student interested in learning which lunch choice is most nutritious in the school cafeteria might collect data, select an appropriate graphic representation, and then use that representation to present his findings to his peers, teachers, and principal. Another student might be interested in the relationship between watching TV and school grades, collect data, and represent the correlation graphically, looking for the most appropriate means to demonstrate the findings. Providing students with opportunities to model different phenomena in the world around them leads to a better understanding of that world and to the mathematical relationships within it.

Does Your Classroom Look Like a Math Classroom?

Creating a classroom that clearly shows the importance of student work related to mathematics is essential in motivating students to create ways to represent their mathematical thinking. Students entering a classroom that visually represents the mathematics being studied are more likely to share in that enthusiasm and be willing to create and share their work. Instead of static commercially produced displays that stay up from September to June, create opportunities for students to display their work or make the displays timely and interactive so that students can draw meaning from the information they contain. Create opportunities for students to share and display their interpretations and applications of the vocabulary words being studied through the use of interactive word walls. Instead of having students routinely copy definitions from the glossary, challenge them to find and present real-world examples of the math vocabulary and math concepts. Once the examples are displayed, other students can see if they can determine which vocabulary word or concept the picture represents.

Creating a Classroom Environment That Encourages Multiple Student Representations

Instead of asking students to define math concepts using the glossary in the back of their text, have them write the definitions in their own words, representing each concept using an illustration of their choice, and finally, adding a real-life application that is appropriate for the concept. Moving the class from copying dictionary definitions to representing concepts in multiple forms is not an easy process. As a class, do several of these together in the beginning, and as students began to feel more comfortable with the process, they look forward to creating those representations, which for them bring real meaning to the mathematics. Each week, generate a list of about three to five terms being discussed during the week or terms that come up in the math lessons. Allow the students to discuss these words in small groups and plan how they think the concepts could best be represented. By working cooperatively on their representations, students begin engaging more and more in math conversations that help other students clarify concepts that for them may still be somewhat fuzzy.

At the same time, students may begin looking for more and more ways to demonstrate the real-life applications of the math for their representations, leading them to search newspapers, magazines, and yes, even their textbooks for examples they could use to illustrate the math concepts. Encourage students to look at home for other sources of information about the concepts and words being defined. This home–school connection may provide a very welcome communication tool that helps parents keep up to date on which topics are covered during the week. By challenging students to find real-life applications, we are now able to have instant wall displays that became sources of conversation around the mathematics.

Teachers can facilitate the process of student representations by creating a classroom that encourages students to represent their math thinking in a variety of ways. One way to encourage a climate of student representation is to provide students with the tools they need to create those representations. Baskets of markers, crayons, and colored pencils to which students have easy access will go a long way in getting students motivated to express their ideas. Because most students in the beginning see representations as drawings, they may be more inclined to create those drawings if they have drawing tools. It would be great if every classroom had unlimited supplies of easel pads so that students could share their representations for the whole class to see, but we all know this isn't the case. One possible solution would be to have bulletin boards covered with brown wrapping paper or any other solid-color paper and allow students to draw their representations directly on the board.

It is also important that students have an opportunity to share with those around them their interpretations of the mathematics and discuss how their representations help them understand and illustrate the concepts. A room that encourages communication is one in which students have the ability to work cooperatively, either in small groups or in pairs. When students have the ability not only to discuss the mathematics with their peers but also to listen to them explain their thinking, they are more likely to bring their own meaning to the concepts at hand.

As students are working on representing their math ideas, consider putting four desks together and then placing a precut piece of bathroom tile board (from your local building supply store) on top of the four desks, creating an instant work space. The tile board (made of melamine) should have the same dimensions as the four desks combined. Any manipulatives students may be using will not fall through the cracks, and more important, with a dry-erase marker, students can create their representations right on the table before they put their finished copy on paper. You can do this for pairs of student desks as well. Students working on the tile board can all do the problem in their own way and then share out from their table. This also makes a great "gallery walk": Students can get up and walk around the room to look at all of the other solutions and representations of the problem.

A note of warning: Consider having the edges of the tile board smoothed (using a router or sandpaper) prior to use to eliminate sharp edges and corners and provide careful supervision as students place them on the top of their desks.

How Can Technology Be Used to Encourage Student Representations?

There are an increasing number of technology options available today that can be used to encourage and facilitate student representations of mathematical thinking. When used by an experienced teacher, technology can not only enhance math instruction, but it can also raise the level of cognitive demand and help students see and experience the connection to real-world applications in a realistic manner. In earlier grades, physical models are used frequently, but as students progress, models may no longer be available that can be used to represent advanced concepts. Computers, graphing calculators, document cameras, interactive white boards, and other emerging technologies are just a few of the tools that can be used in a math classroom to motivate and encourage learners.

Computers can, in some cases, provide virtual manipulatives or opportunities for simulations that model the mathematical processes. By using computers, students have access to a library of shapes and figures that can be manipulated in any number of ways to illustrate a concept. Computers can also offer programs that allow students to take part in simulations that allow them to apply the math concepts being studied.

Because of the complexity of the calculations required at this level, student use of calculators has increased dramatically. The more sophisticated graphing calculator is introduced during the middle grades years, and as students become proficient with its use, they will find additional opportunities to make use of this tool during problem-solving situations. If the focus of the lesson is finding the volume of a cylinder, using a calculator frees up the student to focus on the process instead of the computation.

The flexibility of the graphing calculator allows students to use it not only for computation but also for graphing, creating tables, and applying formulas. With additional software, teachers can create a connected classroom where students' solution can be seen at any time at their teacher station. Interactive white boards provide yet another opportunity for teachers to engage student learners. The boards not only serve as a forum for student-created presentations, but as the mathematics becomes more complex, this technology affords new possibilities for student engagement at a higher level. With the touch of a special stylus or even a finger, shapes, numbers, or words can be moved around the screen to illustrate a solution or problem. Throughout this book, we will examine specific areas where these and other technology options might be used.

How Can the Use of Representations Help All Populations?

Classrooms today are becoming increasingly diverse. With added ELL (English language learner) populations as well as the increasingly inclusive nature of all classrooms, it is more important than ever to meet the needs of a wide range of student abilities. At the same time, as teachers are becoming more cognizant of the research associated with learning styles, finding ways to reach those learners is crucial. Teachers who encourage students to represent their mathematical thinking in a variety of ways can help meet the needs of those students who may find difficulty in explaining

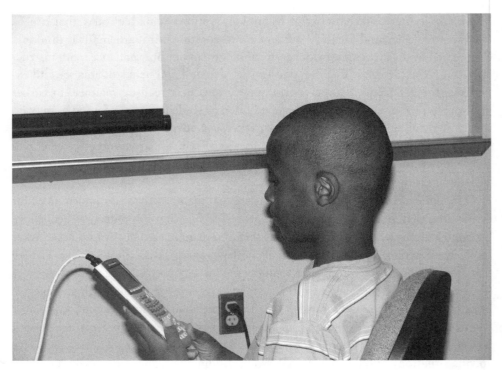

Figure I–2 *The graphing calculator provides students with advanced options in representing their math solutions.*

or writing down their thinking in words. Students who need alternative ways of expressing their thinking often find that pictorial representations open a much-needed path for communication. For example, an ELL student will find it much easier to solve a problem that is presented pictorially rather than written in words. Likewise, a teacher is much more likely to see a student's thinking when the steps in the solution are either drawn out or written in numeric fashion.

The same holds true for special education students working in an inclusive classroom. When the entire class is involved in looking at the math through mathematical models and being encouraged to represent their answers in like fashion, all students feel included and do not feel that they are being singled out for alternative instruction. The key is to have all students feeling comfortable with this process and feeling equal in their ability to understand and communicate the mathematics. Students need to understand that when they are asked to "explain their answer" and "show their work," there are a number of ways they can do so.

CLASSROOM-TESTED TIP

As students become more comfortable in sharing their ideas with others, it is important to make sure all students have an opportunity to participate in an equal fashion. For that reason, equity sticks are a useful tool in any classroom. From a craft department, purchase craft sticks at the beginning of the year and write each student's name on one of the sticks. As you work through a lesson and question the students, reach into the container, pull out an equity stick, and call on the student whose name is written on the stick.

When using the sticks, if you have reluctant learners or shy students who may not want to answer out loud for fear of being wrong, work out a signal with them ahead of time so they can communicate with you as to whether or not they want to answer prior to calling their name. If you see the signal and know the student feels comfortable enough to answer out loud, then no matter whose name is on the stick pulled from the cup, you can call on the reluctant learner. As an added bonus, equity sticks are a great way to help teachers learn student names at the beginning of the year.

Considerations in Lesson Planning

Ongoing attention to lesson design also helps create an environment in which students feel comfortable representing their math ideas with pictures, tables, numbers, or manipulatives. Planning lessons that routinely include higher-order questioning, cooperative group work, and class discussions set the stage for productive representation. The use of manipulatives, the posing of problems, and the reading of math-related literature provide a stimulus for representing math ideas. A balance of whole-group activities, small teacher-led groups, cooperative groups, partner work, and independent tasks provides varied opportunities for students to develop their representation skills.

In planning lessons, it is important to allow enough time for students to explore math ideas and ways to represent those ideas. Asking follow-up questions that uncover students' reasoning or procedures is vital. Posing fewer tasks but allocating time to discuss ideas and solutions builds students' reasoning and problem-solving skills. Structuring assignments with fewer rote tasks and more reasoning helps balance students' skill development. To ensure that students are not hurried, make sure to allow time for them to share ideas with others prior to beginning an independent task or spend a few minutes modeling representations prior to assigning an independent task.

Creating an environment that promotes communication is about modifying our expectations from quiet students to verbal students and from correct answers to reflective thinking. It is about developing a community of learners who respect each other's ideas, whether right or wrong, and who work to support each other in building math understanding.

How This Book Will Help You

This book is designed to help you better understand the representation process standard and its significance. Although the book is specifically designed for teachers in grades 6 through 8 and correlates with math content generally taught at those levels, teachers at other grade levels may find strategies and activity ideas that can be used with their students as well. In each section, the standards are explained and illustrated through a variety of student work samples, and practical ideas are shared for helping students develop their skills in representing mathematical information, as well as tools to assist you in assessing students' representations.

Chapter 1, "How Representations Support Learning," presents a variety of strategies that illustrate the importance of providing students with opportunities to create representations that make the math meaningful to them. The chapter also offers some suggested interpretations teachers might make about the levels of student understanding just from looking at the student representations. In addition, you will find some practical applications for getting at student representations for various strands of mathematics such as the use of Venn diagrams in a variety of problem-solving situations and at various levels of cognitive demand. Logic problems and their significance in helping students organize solutions in a systematic way are discussed.

Chapter 2, "Using Manipulatives to Model and Illustrate Key Math Concepts," takes a closer look at how the use of manipulatives can guide students as they develop their own representations for the math at hand. Manipulatives are a staple in all math classes. Whether these tools are store bought or teacher created, the research is clear on their importance. Whether it is in geometry or algebraic equations, manipulatives can provide students with a model that will help them internalize a concept and then enable them to create their own model and interpretation of the math concept. This chapter also provides classroom examples of how the connection between the concrete manipulative and the student representation can be used to build student understanding.

Chapter 3, "Using Pictures and Diagrams to Represent Mathematical Thinking," takes you through one of the most difficult concepts for students at these grade levels and offers some suggestions on how to use proven instructional strategies to help students clarify concepts and processes related to fractions. Using a key reading strategy such as *before, during, and after*, teachers may find a way to provide their students with an avenue for representing the mathematics that will help them build on prior knowledge and connect that knowledge to new processes.

Chapter 4, "Using Numbers and Symbols to Represent Mathematical Ideas," explores the value of student-invented algorithms as well as ways to use them to support student learning. Moving students from the pictorial to the numeric representation of the mathematics is ultimately the goal in any math classroom, but helping students make the connections and bring meaning to the math is a crucial process and one that cannot be rushed.

Chapter 5, "Using Tables and Graphs to Record, Organize, and Communicate Ideas," discusses developing student understanding of how to graph specific types of data. Whether graphing information on a box-and-whisker plot or a stem-and-leaf plot, students need to understand and see the various data representations used so that they have the skill to choose the appropriate representations for any type of data.

Chapter 6, "Assessing Students' Representations," looks at how teachers can make decisions about assessments as they apply to the representation standard.

Finally, in Chapter 7, "Representation Across the Content Standards," we share lesson ideas to illustrate the representation process standard as it connects to the teaching of numbers and operations, algebra, geometry, measurement, and data and probability. Engaging students in representing their mathematical thinking in all content standards will ensure their success in applying the process in other areas.

At the end of each chapter, we include Questions for Discussion that can be used for individual reflection or to generate faculty study group discussions. The accompanying CD provides a variety of practical resources you can use to help your students more effectively represent their math ideas, including lesson ideas and scoring rubrics, which can easily be adapted to meet your individual needs. This book will expand your understanding of the representation standard and will provide you with the practical resources that you'll need to implement the ideas with your students. You will also be able to take the activities on the CD and personalize them for use in your classroom. All along the way, the Classroom-Tested Tip boxes will provide examples of time-saving, student-motivating, and curriculum-enhancing ideas that come from the classrooms of experienced math teachers. They are designed to make classroom management and instruction a little easier and more meaningful and to send the message that, yes, math can be fun!

Each chapter builds on the previous chapter but can also stand alone if you are looking for one or two ideas to help math instruction in your classroom. As you read through, keep this in mind: This book is written by math teachers for math teachers, with the hope that as you read through the book, at some point in time, you'll have that *aha* moment and you will say to yourself, "That just might work!"

Questions for Discussion

1. What does it mean to say that representation can be both a process and a product?

2. How can representing math ideas help students strengthen their understanding of math?

3. How can attention to students' representations help teachers better assess students' understanding?

4. What are some of the physical characteristics of a math classroom that encourage students to freely represent math ideas?

5. How can students be encouraged to communicate mathematically through representations?

6. How can the classroom environment encourage a climate of student representation?

CHAPTER 1

How Representations Support Learning

The Value of Understanding How to Represent Math Ideas

Stop for a minute, close your eyes, and picture in your mind the one math problem that frustrated you as a student. It made your palms sweat, and even today, just the thought of having to tackle it can cause waves of anxiety. For most of us, it probably has something to do with trains A and B leaving two stations. Imagine now that you are a middle grades student faced with not only those two trains but other problems such as: Jack's sister is three times his age. Twelve years from now, she will be . . . You can finish the problem any number of ways.

The point is that for the average middle grades student, math can be a scary topic. By the time students reach middle grades, most of them fall into two categories: They either like math or they hate it! Students generally like the subject if they have managed to get to middle grades and are still comfortable manipulating the numbers because they have a keen number sense. Students who have successfully put all of the pieces together and understand how to solve problems aren't intimidated by new processes and procedures. However, for those students reaching middle grades still not sure why $7 \times 9 = 63$ or how you add two fractions with unlike denominators, a math class can be pure torture. Many times, those students are on the receiving end of page after page of practice problems designed to improve their understanding of mathematics. What they end up understanding is that if you don't get it, you are going to get more problems.

Then there are those students who still don't understand why they are doing certain procedures, but they have been able to memorize the steps in completing problems. They are good at imitating the process. They aren't sure if their answer makes sense, but they know they have the steps correct. For some students, math just doesn't make sense. Pages of naked math problems aren't going to help with their understanding. On top of their already growing dislike of math, middle grades students now must move from the relative safety of whole-number operations to working with rational and irrational numbers. The problem is now compounded due to the complexities of the numbers themselves. If students have not internalized the whole-number operations or if they have not yet developed their number sense, they unfortunately fall further and further behind.

As middle grades math teachers, what can we do to break the cycle? How can we turn around a negative attitude and help students see the logic and beauty of the mathematics? How can we help them see how the math they are learning in the classroom is connected to their everyday lives and their future careers? At the same time, what is it that we can do to continue to challenge those students who are already successful? It isn't easy being a middle grades math student, and it certainly isn't easy being a middle grades math teacher. There are strategies, however, that can be used in the classroom to help bring meaning to the mathematics. We can help students who may have given up on mathematics see the light at the end of their long tunnel.

One way to help students achieve success in mathematics is to help them develop their skills in representing their ideas as they tackle math problems. When students represent all of their thinking, we can better see if they have any misconceptions about a concept or procedure. Students come to middle grades with a great deal of knowledge; it isn't necessary to start from scratch. Showing students the power of drawing pictures and using numbers and symbols, words, graphic organizers, technology, and manipulatives to bring a sense of understanding to the problems provides them with a strategy that can aid them in approaching any problem. This process can also provide a classroom teacher with invaluable information on where a student falls along the math continuum. The ability to create multiple representations in solving any type of math problem cannot be overestimated. Middle grades students often are not comfortable sharing their attempts at math with others. They have learned to be cautious when it comes to giving answers in a room full of students ready to pounce on an incorrect answer. It is not an easy task, but it is important because students who have the confidence to represent problems in a variety of ways bring a sense of understanding and ownership to the mathematics around them and develop lifelong problem-solving skills that will translate over to other areas.

Organizing Information

Learning to record or represent thinking in an organized way, both in solving a problem and in sharing a solution, is an acquired skill for many students (National Council of Teachers of Mathematics 2000).

How many times have we stood helplessly by and watched a student or group of students try to work through a seemingly easy problem that they have not been able to solve or a problem with multiple solutions? They have either missed the solution(s) because of unorganized trials and errors or failed to see how close they were to the actual solution(s) because of haphazard notations. Perhaps the answer was right in front of their eyes, but because of the disorganized nature of their work, it went unnoticed. This is especially true when the answer is more easily found by discovering a function or pattern in the data that ultimately leads to a solution. Problems with multiple constraints can give students a difficult time if they are not careful to consider the whole problem instead of trying to solve it one part at a time.

Consider the following problem:

Walking down the street, I looked in a store window and saw chairs and three-legged stools. I counted a total of seventy-two legs and twenty-one seats. How many chairs and stools did I see?

This is one of those relatively easy problems for students at this level to solve, but when working on it, students may find it difficult to solve efficiently if they do not make an effort to organize their work in some type of table or matrix. Students would certainly more easily recognize the solution if they used an organizational structure that allowed them to keep track of all of their trials.

Students using a table such as the one in Figure 1–1 would be able to see after a couple of guesses which direction to go with their next guess. Keeping track of and organizing the trials would ultimately lead them to see that each time you decrease the number of chairs and increase the number of stools by the same number, the number of legs decreases. They may not be able to express it in those terms, but that isn't important at this stage of the game. The goal would be to find the solution with fewer guesses but also bring a sense of importance to putting their guesses down in an organizational pattern. True, the first guess is just that—a guess—but understanding how that first guess relates to the problem as a whole and the relationship between the first and second guess to the ultimate solution is paramount. The solution can be found more quickly (always a selling point with students) when they look at the work in a sequential manner instead of putting guesses all over the paper. When the work is organized, the relationship of the parts of the problem is much more evident, bringing real meaning to the mathematics.

There is no doubt that this type of table is useful in recording trials and errors, but it also records for the teacher the thinking that occurred as the students were engaged in solving the problem. Whether they were using manipulatives, drawing pictures, or using another problem-solving tool, the thinking is revealed in the recordkeeping of the trials. Going back and asking, "Do you remember what you were thinking with this guess?" or "Why did you decide to try this number next?" would be impossible if the student didn't keep any record of the trials and errors.

Some students may choose to solve this problem by representing the chairs and the stools pictorially instead of using a matrix of trials. The challenge here is to get

	☒	☒	☑
	Trial 1	**Trial 2**	**Trial 3**
Chairs	15 seats × 4 legs	10 seats × 4 legs	9 seats × 4 legs
Stools	6 seats × 3 legs	11 seats × 3 legs	12 seats × 3 legs
Total Legs	78 legs	73 legs	72 legs
Total Seats	21 seats	21 seats	21 seats

Figure 1–1 *An organized table can help students solve problems.*

at students' thinking as they work through the problem. Unless students make a conscious effort to communicate their trials, there is no way to see the progression of thought. The other downfall of representing the problem pictorially is the time that it takes to arrive at the solution. Encourage students to look at the possibility of creating iconic representations to speed up the process.

When Carileigh approached this problem, she began as most middle grades students do by trying to solve the problem using computation. She started by dividing seventy-two by three, thinking this would give her the number of stools. When she came up with twenty-four, she knew it couldn't be correct because there were only twenty-one seats. She then tried seventy-two divided by four to get eighteen. Since her answer was less than twenty-one, she thought she had found the solution until she began to write out her explanation. With eighteen chairs, she quickly realized that even though she had accounted for all of the legs (seventy-two), she had not used all of the seats. Having students write about their solution after they think they are finished is a powerful tool and allows them an opportunity not only for reflection on their work but also for a reflection on their solution. Middle grades students are just happy to be finished with a problem, and sometimes, they haven't taken the time to analyze the reasonableness of the solution. In this case, Carileigh, by writing about her solution, realized she was not correct and in her last sentence writes, "I got 24 but there can't be. . . . " (See Figure 1–2.)

She stops here to look at her options and decides that since division hasn't worked for her, she needed to try another approach. With some additional help from her classmate Evelyn, the two of them worked on drawing a table that would organize their trials and errors. They started by talking through the problem to make sure they didn't leave anything out. With the table in place, Carileigh went back to her original work and started with the number eighteen. Even though she knew this was not the solution, she wanted to see if the chart would help her decide on the next guess. She placed eighteen in the chart next to the section for chairs and saw that she had used all seventy-two legs but only eighteen seats and still she had no more legs to use for stools. The missing piece in this guess is the fact that she needed to use twenty-one seats and she used only eighteen. Her next step was to place a three in the row for three legs so that she used all of the seats available. Together, the girls decided that they needed a lot more stools to lower the number of legs. This is a key understanding in solving a problem such as this. Seeing how the numbers indicate a direction for the next guess is one of the purposes for using a matrix. Although their third guess didn't get them where they needed to be, they knew they were much closer, so they tried a fourth choice and found that with twelve stools and nine chairs they had used all twenty-one seats and seventy-two legs. (See Figure 1–3.)

By seeing the progression of her solution, you are able to get a sense of not only how she worked through the problem but also how she analyzed what she had done. This is a wonderful process but difficult to evaluate without talking to the student. The challenge here is to get students to represent all of their solutions and the steps in the solution so you can get a good picture (no pun intended!).

Other students in the class approached the same problem differently. They chose to try representing the problem algebraically. If x equals the number of stools and y equals the number of chairs, they reasoned that they should be able to solve the prob-

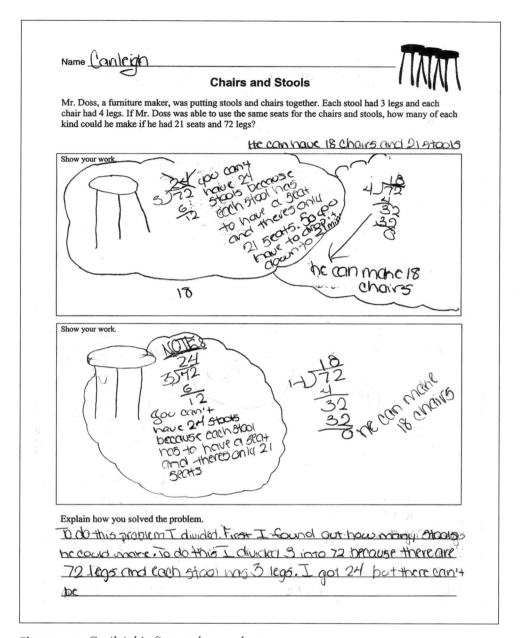

Name ___Carileigh___

Chairs and Stools

Mr. Doss, a furniture maker, was putting stools and chairs together. Each stool had 3 legs and each chair had 4 legs. If Mr. Doss was able to use the same seats for the chairs and stools, how many of each kind could he make if he had 21 seats and 72 legs?

He can have 18 chairs and 21 stools

Show your work.

you can't have 24 stools because each stool has to have a seat and there's only 21 seats. So you have to drop it down to 21 min

18

he can make 18 chairs

Show your work.

NOTES

you can't have 24 stools because each stool has to have a seat and there's only 21 seats

one can make 18 chairs

Explain how you solved the problem.

To do this problem I divided. First I found out how many stools he could make. To do this I divided 3 into 72 because there are 72 legs and each stool has 3 legs. I got 24 but there can't be

Figure 1–2 *Carileigh's first and second attempts*

lem using the equation: $3x + 4y = 72$. Caution needs to be exercised here when allowing students to use equations if they have not fully grasped the importance of looking at the relationships within the problems. Many times, students in the early stages of working with equations will automatically assign different variables to all of the unknowns without looking for connections among the unknowns. In this case, the students set up a table of solutions complete with notes on what they needed to keep in mind as they chose possible answers. (See Figure 1–4.)

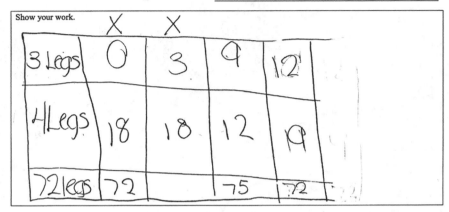

Name **Carileigh**

Chairs and Stools

Mr. Doss, a furniture maker, was putting stools and chairs together. Each stool had 3 legs and each chair had 4 legs. If Mr. Doss was able to use the same seats for the chairs and stools, how many of each kind could he make if he had 21 seats and 72 legs?

_____

Show your work.

	X	X		
3 Legs	0	3	9	12
4 Legs	18	18	12	9
72 legs	72		75	72

Explain how you solved the problem.

To solve this problem I multiplied. I started with 18 legs but that would mean that I would not have room for any stools. Then I tried 12 chairs and 9 stools but that gave me 75 legs. Finally I tried 12 stools and 9 chairs and got 72.

Figure 1–3 *Carileigh's finished work*

Stools	Chairs	Notes from the problem:
X	Y	$x + y$ must equal 21
		$3x + 4y$ must equal 72
20	1	$3 \times 20 + 4 \times 1 = 64$ legs
10	11	$3 \times 10 + 4 \times 11 = 74$ legs
12	9	$3 \times 12 + 4 \times 9 = 72$ legs

Figure 1–4 *Using algebra to solve the problem*

The trials and errors in this case are very similar to the solution shown in Carileigh's matrix, but by bringing in the algebraic representation, these students have demonstrated another degree of understanding to this problem.

The following examples can all be used to help students see a progression of trials and errors as they work through the problems.

1. Walking by a farm, I saw chickens and cows. I counted fifteen heads and forty legs. How many chickens and cows did I see?

2. A bicycle maker was putting together bikes and tricycles. Assuming that the handlebars and wheels could be used on either one, how many of each could he make with fifteen sets of handlebars and thirty-nine wheels?

3. Sue looked out her schoolroom window and saw a group of pigeons and cats. She counted all the legs of the pigeons and cats and found that the total number of legs adds up to sixty-six. How many of each kind of animal (pigeons and cats) passed by her window if the total number of animals was twenty-four?

There are endless possibilities in working with problems of this nature. Students should find the problems easy to represent but also easy to create. Having students solve problems created by classmates adds an element of motivation to the process. It also forces the creator to take care in making sure all of the numbers add up, and students love creating challenges for their fellow classmates.

Another strategy for getting students used to representing and organizing their solutions is with logic problems. Using logic problems in a math classroom gives students an opportunity to practice their step-by-step problem-solving skills. Students engaged in solving logic problems such as those dealing with deductive reasoning skills would find it almost impossible to reach an accurate conclusion in a timely fashion without the use of a table or matrix. It is essential they have the ability to record the information given so that they can start eliminating the impossible situations first. Because most of these problems can be solved without worrying about the math, even students struggling with the subject can level the playing field when it comes to solving these types of problems. Consider the following problem:

Five skiers were finishing a race. From the following information, can you tell how Al, Barbara, and Dion placed in the race?
Carol placed third, and Evan placed second.
Al was not last. Al came in after Evan. Dion was not first.

In this example, students would start with what is given. Therefore, if Al was not last, students could eliminate that choice and also eliminate the first-place choice for Al since the problem states he came in after Evan. Because the problem tells us that Carol placed third and Evan placed second, Al must have come in fourth. The last clue means that Barbara must have come in first since she and Dion are the only possible choices left and the problem tells us that Dion wasn't first. If Barbara came in first, Dion had to finish the race last. Figure 1–5 shows the completed solution. Logic problems such as these hold so much value in training students to start with what is given and then work through the problem step by step before reaching a conclusion. The catch here is getting students to avoid premature conclusions. Some students jump to conclusions before they have sufficient information, and once they make an incorrect assumption, it is almost impossible to correctly finish the problem.

Solving deductive reasoning problems such as these is a much-needed precursor skill for algebra. The value of organizing information during any mathematical situation cannot be overestimated. It is through this process that students bring meaning to the situation and communicate their understanding of the problem at hand. The hard part for students here is communicating solutions in order. Once the problem is finished, do they have any idea what they did first, second, third, or last? Sometimes, sticky notes or highlighter markers can be used to keep track of that information, or students can try to number their steps as they work through the problem.

In Mrs. Robinson's seventh-grade class, deductive reasoning puzzles are done on a regular basis, with students creating the matrices from the problems given. As a part of their regular problem-solving activities, students work either independently or in small groups to create the matrix and work through the problem. Here's an example of the problems they work with:

> Five people play in a band. The instruments include a clarinet, drums, a flute, a saxophone, and a trumpet. The names of the band members are John, Paul, George, Ringo, and Mick. Use the clues to determine who plays what instrument.
>
> ▪ John plays the saxophone.
>
> ▪ George does not play an instrument that uses wind.
>
> ▪ Ringo does not play the flute or the clarinet.
>
> ▪ Paul's instrument is held sideways when it is played.

Students working in small groups set the problem up by first counting the number of categories needed to create the matrix. Joe commented that since there were five people and five instruments, the matrix needs to be six by six. Once students had the grid drawn, they set to work labeling each of the squares. Carla wondered if it mat-

	First	Second	Third	Fourth	Fifth
Al	no	no	no	yes	no
Barbara	yes	no	no	no	no
Carol	no	no	yes	no	no
Dion	no	no	no	no	yes
Evan	no	yes	no	no	no

Figure 1–5 *Matrix for race problem*

tered whether the names went across the top or down the side. Since Mrs. Robinson wanted students to try to answer their own questions, the group decided that as long as one side had the names and the other side had the instruments, it shouldn't matter which side they used for which category. David compared the matrix to a multiplication chart and said that since order didn't matter in a multiplication table, it shouldn't matter here.

The group began putting checks and Xs in the squares as they read the clues. The first check was in the box that intersected John and saxophone, and that meant that an X needed to go in all other boxes in that column and row. Since the problem said George doesn't play an instrument that uses wind, the students put a check in the box for drums. The saxophone had been ruled out for George since it was already determined that John played that instrument. The students put Xs in the flute and clarinet boxes for Ringo and a final check in the box for Paul and flute, since that is the only instrument that is held sideways when it is played. The only other boxes remaining were for Mick and the clarinet and Ringo and the trumpet. The group finished their matrix and shared their response with the rest of the class.

Venn Diagrams

The Venn diagram is another tool that enables students to organize information such as the attributes of shapes, aspects of data, common factors and multiples, or the similarities and differences of numbers and shapes. It is also a valuable tool that can be used in problem-solving situations. Students just beginning work with Venn diagrams can start with a single circle and a question or survey with only two choices: either it is or it isn't. For example, initial work with Venn diagrams would start with topics such as shirts with collars, shirts with no collars; shirts with words or numbers, shirts with no words or numbers; or students who buy lunch, students who pack their lunch. With a single circle, the inside could be one of the two characteristics, and the outside would be the other. Venn diagrams can be made more complex with the addition of more circles, allowing for additional sets or elements to be compared. In multicircle Venn diagrams, each region represents one attribute or characteristic, and the overlapping region of two or more circles represents those attributes the elements have in common. Outside the circles is yet another area that can be used to represent those numbers, shapes, or pieces of data that do not belong to any group.

In addition to determining common characteristics, Venn diagrams can be used to help students with some numeric processes. Students asked to find common factors of two numbers could organize their information using a Venn diagram so that the common factors could be easily recognized, or the diagrams could provide an alternative method of simplifying fractions. Consider the following situation: Find the factors and common factors of twenty-four and thirty-six. Using a Venn diagram such as the one in Figure 1–6, students would first identify the factors of twenty-four and place them in circle A. The factors of thirty-six would be placed in circle B. Any factor found in both circles would then be placed in the region where the two circles overlapped.

Students using this Venn diagram would have no trouble picking out the common factors as well as the greatest common factor (GCF), twelve. This organizational

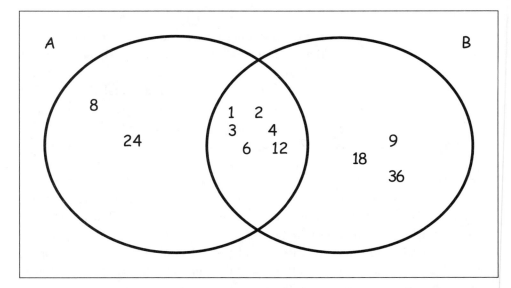

Figure 1–6 *Venn diagram showing the factors of twenty-four and thirty-six*

tool works in a number of situations, such as solving computational problems involving fractions needing common denominators, but it is made more powerful when students have an opportunity to choose the attributes or characteristics each circle will represent.

The Venn can also be rotated so that it looks like one circle in on top of the other. (See Figure 1–7.) In this example, students can use the Venn to help determine whether a fraction has been stated in the simplest form. For example, if the students were looking at the fraction twelve-fifteenths, they would start by doing the prime factorization for both numbers. Once they had the factors of both, they would put them in the diagram, with the common factors in the middle.

Since both numbers have a prime factor of three, that number would go in the intersection of the two circles, as in Figure 1–7, with the remaining numbers going in the individual sections of each circle. If a section had more than one prime factor, you would multiply them to find the product of those factors.

The end result would be a fraction in its simplest form, four-fifths, since three is the common factor. Using this representation, students can visualize the process of what it means to factor numbers and how the common factors can be removed from the original numbers.

Geometry is another area where students can make use of the Venn diagram. Working with attribute blocks, pattern blocks, or geometric shapes, students could be instructed to place the pieces in one of the regions of the Venn diagram using criteria that they establish. Not only do they have to choose the attributes by which to sort the shapes, but they also have to be able to communicate those decisions to someone looking at their organizer.

It is important to remember to give students the opportunity to make these decisions and allow time for the communication instead of always giving them the characteristics of each area of the Venn. Even though a student's thinking might not always

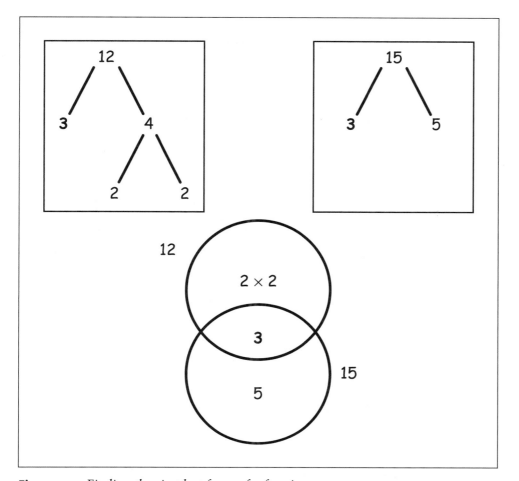

Figure 1–7 *Finding the simplest form of a fraction*

be what we were expecting, there is so much value in allowing students time to work through all of these steps and process their own decisions. It is important for students to identify the attributes of these geometric shapes that create the similarities and differences and determine if there are other ways to group the shapes. One important question to ask would be, "What criteria did you use in placing the shapes outside the Venn?" Students need to feel confident that when they make these decisions and communicate them appropriately, they will be accepted. The vocabulary now becomes more meaningful for the students because they have had time to internalize the concept. It is important for teachers to encourage and accept multiple answers in situations such as this so that students feel more comfortable thinking outside the box. It also provides additional opportunities for those teachable moments we all love.

Once students have had ample opportunities to work with the Venn diagram in multiple problem-solving situations, you can increase the level of difficulty by adding a third circle to the diagram, similar to the one in Figure 1–8. Problems using a third circle can be challenging to say the least, and it is important for the teacher to model their use at first before turning students loose on their own.

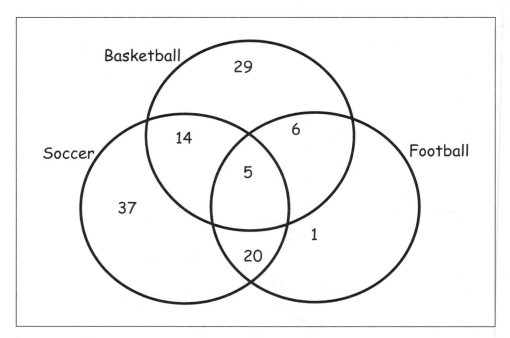

Figure 1–8 *Three-circle Venn diagram*

Students in Mrs. Harbinson's seventh-grade class tackled the following problem during a whole-class activity:

Seventh-grade students completed a survey of the after-school sports they played. According to the survey, a total of fifty-four students played basketball, thirty-two students played football, and seventy-six students played soccer. If fourteen of those students played just basketball and soccer, six played just basketball and football, twenty played just football and soccer, and five students played all three sports, how many students played just one sport?

Naturally, the students immediately started adding and subtracting numbers, forgetting for a moment the tool that they were working with in this case was the triple Venn diagram. Their teacher quickly reminded them that since they had the diagram, they needed to first look at the information that was given and fill in the sections that they could. The students started by labeling the three circles "football," "basketball," and "soccer" and then putting the totals in each of the portions of the intersecting circles. Then they worked their way to the outside circles for the final answers. As they worked their way to the outside sections, they had to remember to continue to include the previous numbers in their totals. For example, since five students played all three sports, the students had to remember to include those five students in the totals for each of the three sports. They also needed to include the students playing two sports in each of the totals for the individual sports. The final count for individual sports was thirty-seven students played just soccer, twenty-nine students played just basketball, and only one student played just football. Mrs. Harbinson asked them to go back to the original question and check their answers to make sure they had not counted a student twice. Bruce's group showed their check as follows:

Statement 1: Fifty-four students played basketball. Our numbers: 29 + 14 + 5 + 6 = 54 ✓

Statement 2: Thirty-two students played football. Our numbers: 20 + 5 + 6 + 1 = 32 ✓

Statement 3: Seventy-six students played soccer. Our numbers: 14 + 5 + 20 + 37 = 76 ✓

They then checked their Venn diagram against the remaining numbers, and since no numbers needed to be added, they concluded that they had checked everything needed.

An added challenge to this type of problem would be to have students start with the numbers for each sport and pairs of sports and then determine the total number of students in the survey.

C L A S S R O O M - T E S T E D   T I P

If you are looking for a way to add a little fun to the use of the Venn diagram and meet the needs of some of your more kinesthetic learners, hula hoops make great Venn diagram circles. Even middle grades students enjoy the opportunity to work with problems in unconventional ways. The hoops can be placed on the floor or attached to the chalkboard. Students can represent their answers by putting the shapes, numbers, cards, manipulatives, or themselves inside the circles. If your chalkboard is also magnetic, attach small magnets to the back of the cards, and students can take turns placing answers in the appropriate sections. Purchasing a roll of magnetic tape and cutting it into pieces is an economical way to accomplish this task. This is a great way to get students up and moving!

Recording Ideas or Observations

Students actively engaged in creating their own notes and observations bring a keen sense of understanding to the mathematics, as opposed to students copying teacher-created notes. For students to construct their own knowledge and understandings about the mathematics, they need to be active participants. Passive learners aren't working to create new ideas and connections, and while it is sometimes easier just to give students the information as they work through an investigation, the only person constructing meaning from the material in that case is the teacher. We can't tell students how to think; we can't be the authors of their ideas and observations. What we can do is create a community of mathematicians that sees value in being able to connect information, gleaned from investigations or experiments, to the abstract mathematical concepts that will make them successful in connecting to skills and concepts with a higher level of cognitive demand. To this end, we need to encourage students to observe, process the information, and note what is important to remember. Easier said than done! How do you create this community of self-assured mathematicians eager to observe and record with the eye of an investigative reporter?

One way is to provide an early note-taking structure to classroom lessons or investigations and encourage students to develop a system of representations that makes sense to them. Students can be supported in the beginning with templates that allow them ways to zero in on what's important. A chart, a diagram, or a set of guiding questions to ask as they work through the process goes a long way toward helping them develop good mathematical communication.

As students are working on new material, have them set their paper up in two columns. One column could be for the examples, and the second column could be the work section, or one column could be set up for note taking, and the second column for examples and pictorial representations of the vocabulary.

When students are presented with new vocabulary, the Frayer model encourages a variety of representations. Named for Frederick Frayer, this is an activity that gives students an opportunity to study vocabulary by looking at the relationships of the concept's attributes. Students divide their paper into four sections. On one section, they write a student-created or glossary definition of the word, and in a second section, they create an example or examples of that word. In the third section, they can draw a picture or diagram of the term, and in the fourth section, students can describe a real-world application. Giving students the opportunity to relate the mathematics to a real-world application is important for long-term retention. Without the connection, the math is sometimes forgotten. Alternative categories include creating sections of examples and sections of nonexamples. By allowing students an opportunity to create nonexamples, we are encouraging them to internalize the important characteristics of the concept at hand and identify what must be included to make an example. In Figure 1–9, a student has used the Frayer model to illustrate the concept of acute angles. The student identified the characteristics of acute angles but also included some nonexamples that to them represented other types of angles.

Another way to bring structure to students' work and help them organize it is to provide note-taking structure that relates to the concept or, in this case, a math-related literature piece.

CLASSROOM-TESTED TIP

Use plastic trays or plates made from melamine for students to record their answers. Using a dry-erase marker, students can write directly onto the surface of the plate. This brings an unexpected element of fun to the activity. The writing wipes right off, and inexpensive sets of white socks work great as erasers. The sock is also a handy place to store the marker, and small plates and markers can be stored in zip-top bags for future use. Smooth placemats also work for an activity like this, although you may find you need to use dry-erase spray to eliminate the shadow marks from the surface once you erase. You'll find many uses for these plates, and seasonal plates and placemats can add an extra dimension of fun to the activity.

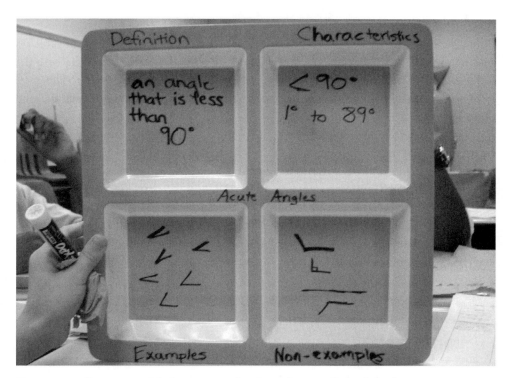

Figure 1–9 *Frayer model shows a student's understanding of angles.*

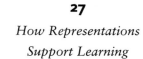

Perimeter and area are two of those related concepts that students always seem to confuse. One reason may be the way the two concepts are taught. Most curricula present the two concepts in tandem because of their relationship to one another. Do our students have enough experiences with one concept before we introduce the second concept? What if students had multiple opportunities to experience activities with only perimeter before we introduced area? Brain research tells us that students who are actively engaged in constructing meaning are more likely to retain and internalize that information. For this reason, providing students with meaningful tasks that require them to interact with the mathematics in a variety of settings will ensure students can transfer that knowledge to higher-level skills.

A wonderful story for reinforcing the skill of recording ideas as students work through a problem is *Spaghetti and Meatballs for All!* by Marilyn Burns (1997). It is a story about a couple wanting to have a dinner for their friends and family. As the story progresses, the number of available seats (perimeter) changes, but the number of tables (area) remains constant. Activities related to this book can engage students in thinking about the way area and perimeter are related to one another and how a change in one may or may not change the other. Using this book with students also provides a real-world application of the concepts. As students listen to the story, they should be provided with manipulatives that simulate the tables and chairs. One favorite manipulative for this activity would be small square crackers used to represent the tables and bear cookies to represent the chairs. Because the situation changes from one page to the next, it is important for students to record the situations as they change. Using large-grid graph paper, students can draw the table-and-seat arrangements from one page to the next. The discussion that takes place after the story ends is crucial to making sure students conceptualize the differences in the two concepts. Questions might include, "What happens to the number of seats when the first set of tables is pushed together?" Students can be prompted to compare the number of tables with the number of seats without making reference to the words *area* and *perimeter*. The hope here is that students will be able to make the important connection between the two concepts using a real-world example.

The Sir Cumference series of books also provides examples on how literature can be used to make the classroom math connection to real-world measurement concepts. In *Sir Cumference and the First Round Table* by Cindy Neuschwander and Wayne Geehan (2002), Sir Cumference, his wife Lady Di, and their son Radius embark on a challenge to create a table for the knights of Sir Cumference. As students read the various books, they should be encouraged to take notes that represent the concepts presented. Students looking to differentiate and remember the various concepts of circles such as diameter and radius will find this literature connection helpful.

CLASSROOM-TESTED TIP

Using a document camera with a projector allows all students to see and experience the math-literature connections that so many books now have. By placing the book under the camera, all students have a clear view of the text and colorful pictures.

Communicate, Communicate, Communicate (aka Write It Down Because I Can't See Inside Your Head!)

One of the most frustrating phrases for a math teacher to hear is, "I don't know how I did it. I just did it in my head." Trying to pull those thoughts and ideas out of our students' heads and getting them down on paper can be a challenging task to say the least. The trick here is to make it meaningful and somewhat fun for the students to communicate their thinking. Engaging students in opportunities to express their ideas and solutions in alternative ways can provide the motivation needed to get the ideas on paper and also accentuate the strengths of diverse learners.

When students are given a problem to solve or challenge to investigate, we can encourage them to do the representation in a number of different ways. For example, one group of students could be challenged to solve the problem strictly using an appropriate algorithm; another group can show the solution pictorially using an iconic symbol or more realistic picture; another group might be challenged to find a way to chart the solution; and of course, other groups could use manipulatives to represent the solution. Student groups can then report to the rest of the groups using their given representation style. Those presentations can bring about choruses of "I didn't think of that" and "That way looks way easier than our way. I'm going to try it that way next time."

Obviously, not all problems lend themselves to solutions with a single representation; however, students should be provided with opportunities to see how a particular representation can be used to make the problem more meaningful. Keep in mind that middle grades students are not overly enthused about drawing pictures or diagrams to solve a problem because they think they can solve the problem with much less work using computation. What happens sometimes is that once the computation is complete, an important step is often skipped, and that is reflection. Unless students take time to reflect on their answer, as Carileigh did in an earlier problem, they seldom see if their solution is reasonable. In their mind, they are finished, and an important piece of the understanding is missed.

In Mrs. Seay's eighth-grade class, the importance of recording representations is reinforced using the classic Moving Traffic problem. In this problem, six cars are positioned in spaces facing one another with three on each side. The object is to get the cars to the opposite side of the lot in as few moves as possible. The conditions for the moves include only one car per space at any given time, and cars can only move forward by sliding to an empty space or jumping over a car to an empty space.

On the surface, this may seem like an easy task and one devoid of mathematics, but the problem can be completed at a number of different levels of difficulty and the mathematics is rich. Taking the problem to a higher level of difficulty and bringing in an understanding of the abstractness of algebra can involve having students work to calculate the fewest number of moves possible for any given number of cars.

In this lesson, Mrs. Seay provides all students with their own set of materials. As students start to work problems such as this and the answer is not easily determined, it is important to allow them time to internalize the task first on an individual basis. If we have students begin in a small-group situation, we run the risk of having students give up and letting others take over the solution phase. The materials used in this problem can be die cuts of cars or any other two-color or two-shaped objects, including two-color counters or square color tiles. The drawback with the two-color counters and tiles is remembering the direction the shapes are headed in because you only want them going forward.

As Mrs. Seay goes over the problem, she cautions the students to read the conditions carefully and experiment with different moves. She also reminds them that unless they can replicate their steps in the solution, they may not consider the problem solved. In other words, it isn't enough just to get the cars to the other side; you have to document the moves in such a way that would allow you to follow the steps when you repeat the process. Her only hint to the students is that they might want to try the problem with fewer cars and spaces first to see if they make any discoveries that might help them with the larger problem. Several students begin moving their cars jumping and rolling to the empty spaces. A few hands go up as students ask what happens when no cars can move forward or what happens if they can't move a particular car. Her answer to all of these questions is to tell them to reread the conditions, and if the conditions cannot be met, then they need to start again.

After the students work with their individual cars for a period of time, Mrs. Seay moves them to small groups. By now, each student has tried the problem at least one or two times, and they each have a sense of what needs to happen, but as of yet, no solution has been found. Since each person in the group still has their individual sets of materials, the group can work together, but each member can replicate the steps using their own materials. Here again, this keeps all members of the group engaged in the problem. Ryan's group is the first to announce a finished product. With high fives all around the group, they are quick to cheer their victory. Since Mrs. Seay sees no evidence of their recordkeeping, she is certain they cannot repeat the steps and explain the process to the class, and as the group tries to show everyone else how the problem is done, they too realize that they didn't record their moves. Without this record, they are unable to share their solution.

This provides a valuable lesson to the other groups, and everyone begins a discussion of how to keep track of their solution. Ryan's group sets up their recording system so that moves are labeled R for rolls and J for jumps. They also decide that they need to indicate the color of the car moving so that when the red car rolls one space, it is recorded RR, and when the yellow car rolls, it is YR. They decide not to worry about the direction the cars are moving because they can go in only one direction. But they determine they need to show which car is moving, so they number them one to three on each side. The number one cars are closest to the empty center spot, and the number three cars on both sides are on the outside.

Their solution (see Figure 1–10) shows how they used a method of representation to show the steps in such a way as to allow anyone else a complete picture of the solution.

Each group has now moved through several different stages within this problem. First, they read the information and worked independently trying to manipulate their cars to the other side of their spaces, and then in small groups, they worked together to reach a solution. As a group, they decided on a system of recording moves to be replicated by others. The final stage in this part of the problem was to direct six classmates to repeat the solution either using their manipulatives or by acting out the problem. One member of the group called out the steps while the other classmates duplicated the steps with their materials.

Mrs. Seay began to ask a series of questions, "Was fifteen the fewest number of moves possible with six cars?" "What happens when only two cars or four cars are used?" "Can you use the information you have gathered to reach an answer about the number of moves possible with any number of cars?" "What about creating an expression that could be used for an unknown number of cars?" Without the representation and the recordkeeping, it would be almost impossible to see the relationships among these situations, but having students realize the importance of accurate recording of information was an important goal of this lesson.

Whatever method students use to show their solution, the key is getting it out of their heads and on the paper. Initially, students will have great difficulty with this skill. With the manipulatives on their desk and the solution in their heads, a teacher will need to coax them to write the solution on the paper. One strategy that works well in cooperative groups is to designate the recorder to write down not only the final answer but also the steps in the process. The more opportunities students have to practice this process and the more opportunities they have to see alternative solution representations, the more likely they are to feel comfortable about their abilities to put their thinking on paper. Students possessing these skills are more apt to tackle problems at a higher level of demand.

Name _____

Traffic Jam

The parking lot has seven spaces and six cars. Only one space can be empty at any time. The task is to get the cars on the left side of the parking lot over to the right hand side while moving the cars on the right over to the left. Cars can only roll over to the next space if it is empty or they can jump over a car if the space on the other side is empty. Since these cars have no reverse, they cannot move backwards.

The object is to move the cars in as few moves as possible. Keep track of your moves so that someone else could follow your steps and repeat the process.

Show your solution.

1 – 1y✓	6. 3y✓	11. 2y)
2 – 1R)	7. 1R)	12. – 3y)
3 – 2RR	8. 2R)	13 – 2RR
4 – 1y)	9. 3R)	14. –3R)
5 – 2y)	10. 1y✓	15. 3yR

15 moves

Figure 1–10 *One group's representation for the Moving Traffic problem*

Using Representations to Model a Process or Concept

It is important to remember that students must be able to construct meaning and internalize the many mathematical processes and concepts that they are expected to learn. Only through that internalization of the process will it ever go beyond the rote memorization level that we all know results in, "Our teacher didn't teach us that last year!" What they really mean is that it was taught, but they just don't remember. We spend a great deal of time chastising the teachers in the previous grade levels for not making sure students knew their multiplication tables, how to divide, or how to add and subtract fractions instead of reflecting on our own practice. Are we guilty of doing the same things? Students provided with opportunities to internalize a process through modeling problem-solving situations instead of just practicing the process over and over again are much more likely to remember and apply the process when confronted with higher-level problems. "Students need to work with each representation extensively in many contexts as well as move between representations in order to understand how they can use a representation to model mathematical ideas and relationships" (NCTM 2000).

Grades 6 through 8 are critical years for students as they refine and extend their skills with whole numbers to working with rational numbers. One of the most widely used manipulative models for place value is base ten blocks. One of the reasons these work so well is that they are already proportional in size and come with ready-made grouped sets of tens, hundreds, and thousands. Students using these models to learn addition, subtraction, and place value can literally see the relationships between the values by comparing the sizes of the pieces. Trading in ten 1s for one 10 or ten 10s for one 100 becomes more meaningful because of the size relationship of the pieces. The physical size of the pieces can serve as a cue to the number relationship between the values.

However, that same model becomes more difficult to use in grades 6 through 8 once the numbers students are working with become larger and more complex. There are times when students can be encouraged to make the problem smaller, but that is sometimes not appropriate for the work at hand. It is important to find ways to help students generalize the magnitude of numbers and place values beyond what they can see with the standard manipulative models. For this reason, we need to engage them in activities that showcase the size of large numbers, and at the same time, we need to make sure they can relate to the size of those numbers that are less than one.

Another manipulative that is not as widely used as the base ten blocks are Digi Blocks™. While they are primarily found in elementary classrooms, their inclusion in a middle grades classroom for those students not yet fully understanding the relationships among 10s, 100s, and 1,000s can be very useful. The blocks themselves can be renamed to different powers of ten so that decimal concepts can be studied, and because the blocks disassemble, students can see the size relationship of the individual sections.

Developing number sense during the intermediate grades using the models at hand can help students as they work with larger numbers, but generalizations are not enough. How many classes have started collecting 1 million bottle caps only to find that the task was too unwieldy or just impossible from a standpoint of finding some place to store the collected caps? Perhaps an easier activity would be to collect 10,000, then 100,000, and then work to help students generalize the number using the grouping model. As students collect the bottle caps, they need to find a system for keeping track of the amounts. Using tally marks allows students to group quantities of the items as they are collected and then translate the symbolic representation to numeric representation. A number of literature books, such as Jerry Pallotta's *Count to a Million* (2003), David Schwartz's *How Much Is a Million?* (1993), and Helen Nolan's *How Much, How Many, How Far, How Heavy, How Long, How Tall Is 1,000?* (2001), focus on larger quantities and help students gain a true sense of the size of those numbers. Using these books in a math classroom helps make that ever important math-literature connection. Additional titles are listed in the Resources for Teachers section of this book.

The Role of the Teacher

One of the most important points we need to remember about graphic organizers or any other organizational tool students might use is that they need to see how the tool can be used for multiple purposes. For example, if students see a Venn diagram used only in reading class for comparing and contrasting, they won't be likely to use it in math class. Seeing the similarities and differences in math concepts and processes is a crucial step in helping students remember and internalize them. Students duplicating an organizer in the same manner that they have seen it modeled may be getting meaning from that process. On the other hand, they may just be copying what they have seen the teacher produce. Allow students an opportunity not only to see various organizers in use but also to choose which ones they want to use for a given situation.

Figure 1–11 *Students work to complete elements of vocabulary using the Frayer model.*

Questions for Discussion

1. Venn diagrams and matrices help students organize their thoughts and trials as they work through problem-solving situations. What other graphic organizers lend themselves to this best practice?

2. What other benefits can be found in making the math-literature connection?

3. What problems encourage students to respond using multiple representations?

4. How can graphic organizers be used to differentiate a problem-solving situation?

5. How can manipulatives be incorporated into a middle grades classroom?

CHAPTER 2

Using Manipulatives to Model and Illustrate Key Math Concepts

Mathematical representations help provide students with a perspective on phenomena.

—Sara P. Fisher and Christopher Hartmann, "Math through the Mind's Eye"

Modeling Ideas with Manipulatives

The National Council of Teachers of Mathematics recommends that teachers should employ "representations to model and interpret physical, social, and mathematical phenomena" (NCTM 2000, 70) and that students should use mathematical representations to organize their thinking and reflect on numeric or geometric information. In Chapter 1, we discussed how different representations support mathematical learning. As students become more comfortable creating models of their thinking, they build a repertoire of strategies from which to select when faced with a novel task. "The very act of generating a concrete representation establishes an image of the knowledge in students' minds," write Marzano et al. (2001). In this chapter, we look at the power of using manipulatives to help students develop their own understanding of mathematical concepts, as well as the role of the teacher in developing meaningful, appropriate tasks with manipulatives.

It isn't easy getting middle grades students to use manipulatives, and it isn't easy getting them to use the manipulatives correctly. Students are interested in shortcuts, and they have learned by now that manipulatives take time. They have also learned that manipulatives can be used for any number of things other than what was intended. Teacher management is important in the use of manipulatives. If students are to be successful in using these materials, routines and procedures need to be in place; otherwise, chaos becomes the order of the day.

Most middle grades students prefer solving a problem with an algorithm. For some of them, it isn't important if the answer is reasonable. If they have an answer, they consider the problem solved. Getting them to take time to reflect on their answer and confirm the answer's reasonableness is not something students do without encouragement. Our challenge is to show them how the manipulatives can be useful in solving a problem and also to help them make sense of the problem. At the middle grades level, manipulatives that are truly useful can be difficult to find. With larger numbers, decimals, fractions, and integers, we need to choose carefully how we incorporate their use into the lesson and by all means keep in mind how important it is to move students to the representation phase with the manipulatives still in hand. Whether we use two-color counters for integer operations, fraction towers, or algebra tiles, students can benefit greatly by using these models to develop their own understandings of the concepts. If students are more comfortable with their own representations, then by all means allow them.

Two words that strike fear into the heart of any sixth-grade student are *decimals* and *fractions*. Worse yet, we all know that students' fear is nothing compared to the fear felt by the middle grades math teacher charged with teaching decimals and fractions. How can we make sense of numbers that are not easily represented using manipulatives? How can we help students understand the complexities of decimals and their decreasing value as they move away from zero? And can we represent fractions with something other than pizza, circles, and rectangles?

Building Understanding through the Use of Manipulatives

When students can see and manipulate ideas, they gain a better understanding of those ideas. The distributive property is often presented as a series of isolated operations to be performed to exact a final answer. Generally speaking, it isn't the computation that trips up the students when it comes to the use of the distributive property; it is remembering to multiply both terms in the parentheses by the value outside the parentheses. If students are going to make an error, it is in forgetting this step. Using a manipulative such as algebra tiles, students are able to connect the concrete representation to the numeric solution and thereby increase their level of understanding as to why the computations are performed. The tiles can be very helpful in aiding student understanding of algebraic concepts such as operations with polynomials, and because they are tactile, many students find it easier to remember otherwise forgotten procedures. They aren't usually used for instruction until middle grades, and for that reason, initial work with this manipulative needs to start at the very basic level. They won't make algebra easy, but they can aid students who up to now have had little understanding due to the abstractness of the course.

The tiles come in packages of different size pieces, and there are mats that can be used when working with the tiles in factoring or operations. Each piece has two colored sides used to represent positive and negative values. The negative side is represented in red, and the other side may be green or in some cases white. The small square pieces are generally called the 1s unit, and the long rectangles are labeled x with the large square shapes called x^2. For the purposes of working with the distributive property at this early stage, it may only be necessary to work with the long rectangles (x) and the small squares (1). Unless integers are to be a part of the expressions, it isn't necessary to talk about the representation of the two colors.

Consider the following task.

Represent $3(x + 2)$ and $3x + 6$. Are they equivalent?

Given a problem such as this, a student would first look at the $x + 2$, and because the quantity is multiplied by 3, they would start by making three sets of $x + 2$. (See Figure 2–1.) Once students have the first expression represented, they can then move to the second expression and represent $3x$ with three of the long rectangles, and using six of the ones units, they have two equivalent expressions. Students can use the tiles to model several different examples using the distributive property, and once integers are introduced, the tiles become another useful manipulative for work with expressions or equations using variables and integers.

When our students are learning about naming fractions, we should allow them to explore this concept with different models. We can give them a set of fraction circles or squares (or both) and a set of two-color counters and the direction to find all the different ways to show one-half. Students will begin to see that in each case, although fractions named one-half may not look the same, they cover the same area of the whole (in this case, one of two equal parts).

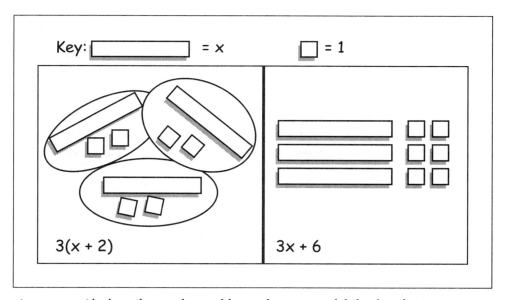

Figure 2–1 *Algebra tiles can be used by students to model the distributive property.*

Figure 2–2 *A student's early work with algebra tiles*

There are three models of fractions we want our students to be familiar with and comfortable using: area/region, length/measurement, and set. Consider the following task:

Choose a fraction model (area/region, length/measurement, or set) to represent each of the following situations. *Explain why you chose the model you did.*

- Beth's plant is $3\frac{1}{4}$ inches tall. Judy's plant is twice as tall. How tall is Judy's plant? (length/measurement model)

- Bennett Middle's sixth-grade classes are planting a vegetable garden. They decide to use one-third of the garden to grow tomatoes. In one-fourth of the garden, they will grow corn, and in another fourth, they will grow beans. In the remaining section, they will grow herbs. Show how you could represent all areas of the garden. What fraction of the garden will be planted with herbs? (area/region model)

- Mr. Kasik's students are on their way to lunch. There are twenty-four students in the class. One-third of the children brought their lunch from home, one-half of the children are buying their lunch, and the remaining students are absent. What fraction of the class is absent today? (set model)

Each of these situations can be best represented by a particular fraction model. We want our students to be experienced enough with the different models so that they can correctly choose the best representation for a fraction situation.

Work fractions and percentages into your everyday language. After giving whole-group instructions, look for table groups to be ready and describe their representation in different ways:

- I see one-fourth of James's table is ready.

- Vincent's table is 33 percent away from being ready.

- Look, 100 percent of Gabriela's table is ready!

Moving from the Concrete to the Abstract

Several cautions need to be kept in mind with the use of manipulatives. The number one mistake we sometimes make in using manipulatives is in structuring student use of manipulatives. Are the students merely copying the steps that we have given them, or are they truly using the manipulative to spur their thinking and reflection on the concept? If students are manipulating algebra tiles by following a series of steps that we set up, then no thought is going into why they are getting the end result, and the manipulative becomes an "answer-getting" tool. The other error that is sometimes made is in transitioning between the concrete and the algorithm. Because manipulatives only provide models for concepts, it is up to the student to construct the meaning. By constructing meaning, the student can then apply the concept to abstract thinking. For this reason, it is important to transition to the abstract while the manipulative is still on the desk. For example, in using two-color counters or number lines to model addition or subtraction of integers, students need to see how the models translate to symbolic representations. Forget for a moment the rules and terms such as absolute value, but begin instead with the context of the problem, the model at hand, and the numeric representation.

Consider the following task to be done with a number line and/or two-color counters.

At noon, the temperature was 18°F. By midnight, the temperature had dropped to –6°F. What was the total difference in temperature?

The number line (see Figure 2–3) representation for this problem shows one bar stretching from zero to 18 to show the first temperature. The temperature starting point is technically 18 for this question, and it must drop to zero before the negative side of the bar can be used to represent that value. The second bar over the number line stretches to –6 because that is the temperature at midnight.

Since the number line shows a total change in temperature to be the sum of 6 and 18, the answer found using the number line is 24°. At this point, students may be

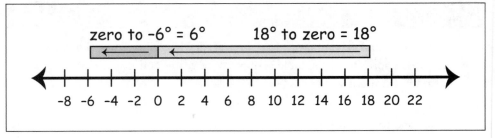

Figure 2–3 *A number line model for integer operations*

totally confused as to how the algorithm applies to this problem. They understand that the only way to get 24 out of this problem is to add the two numbers, but why is the answer 24? It is very tempting to just reveal to the students that they need to change the subtraction sign to an addition sign and make the negative 6 a positive 6. Holding students accountable for understanding a process may require multiple models. Mrs. Melson gave this problem to her seventh-grade prealgebra students and asked them to use their two-color counters to model the solution found on the number line. Working in groups of three or four, the students began putting their counters on their desk to show 18.

> Note: Most counters will either be yellow and red or white and red. Generally speaking, the red side always is used to represent negative values.

Tia raised her hand to let Mrs. Melson know that her group had found the answer. She explained to the class, "Because we have 18 white counters for the 18° and 6 red counters for the –6°, that makes 24 counters, so our answer matches the number line."

Steve's hand shot in the air, and he immediately said that the solution Tia explained couldn't possibly be correct because you can't count negatives and positives together. He continued, "Just because you have 24 counters doesn't mean you have

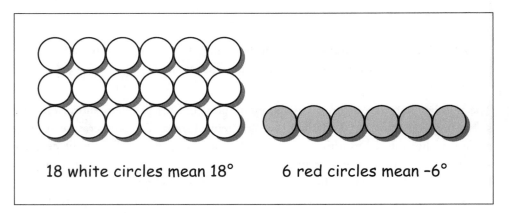

Figure 2–4 *Using two-color counters to solve an integer problem*

24. The red counters can't be counted with the white counters. They aren't the same thing." Several other students in the class agreed with Steve, but there were still others not sure. Mrs. Melson asked them to go back to their problems, and if Tia's solution was not correct, how would students get the answer to this question? She wasn't ready to tell them how to find a solution or even if Tia's group had the right solution because so many of them still did not see how the numbers in the problem matched the number line and the counters. Steve raised his hand to say that he thought he had the answer.

He started with Tia's original representation of the problem and laid out 18 white counters to represent 18°. He said, "I know I have to start with 18 and I know I have to subtract 6° because subtraction means you move backward on the number line, and going from a positive temperature to a negative is a backward move." He continued with, "I don't have any negatives to take away from the 18° since they are all positive, but I can add 6 zeros without changing the value of 18."

Tia wasn't convinced that adding 6 more counters wasn't going to change the value, so she said, "I don't think you can just add 6 more counters because you want to."

Mrs. Melson placed 12 counters under the document camera and asked the students to tell her how many counters she had. She had 6 red counters and 6 white counters. One student raised her hand to say 12 while another student said that because for every red counter there was a white counter, the total value of the counters was zero. Mrs. Melson went through a few more examples before she directed them back to Steve's solution, and she asked, "How many counters does Steve have, and what is the value of the counters?" At this point, she emphasized the difference between number of counters and their value because she wanted everyone to be clear on what was being asked. Tia responded that there were 30 counters, but the value of the counters was still 18 since only pairs of zeros had been added. With everyone on the right track, Mrs. Melson asked Steve to continue with his explanation. He said now that he had negative counters, he could take away 6 of them leaving 24 white counters, which represented the 24° from the problem so the problem was $18 - (-6)$ and the answer was 24. (See Figure 2–5.)

One of the confusions that arises from a problem such as this is in choosing the correct operation. Many students will not be confident in knowing whether to add or

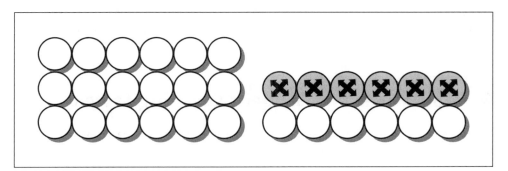

Figure 2–5 *Subtracting integers using two-color counters*

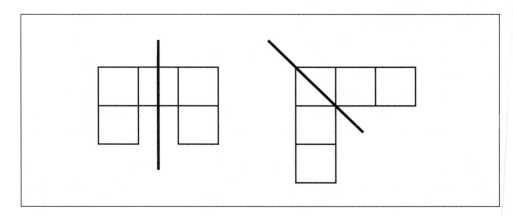

Figure 2–6 *Example figure showing symmetry*

subtract. The word *difference* in the question provides a clue, and most students will know that this is a clue for subtraction, but students may still struggle as they work to reconcile the algorithm to the context. Remember, students are still trying to relate and apply computational strategies they have learned in the past to this new knowledge. Problems with integers provide conflicting results, and students would rather put down a numeric answer than represent the problem in a diagram or use a manipulative. In this case, Mrs. Melson chose to use not only a number line but the two-color counters as well, giving her students a choice as to which representation helped with their understanding.

Another concept that can be difficult for students is symmetry. How many times do we give students a picture and say, "Draw the lines of symmetry"? By manipulating tiles, pattern blocks, and other objects, students can explore the concept of symmetry in an engaging way, as seen in the following task:

> Use your color tiles (or tangrams, pattern blocks, pentominoes, etc.) to design figures that show symmetry. Sketch your figures on the page below. Draw a line (or lines) to show the line(s) of symmetry. (See Figure 2–6.)

Again, students are asked to complete a task using concrete materials, and then they must move toward a more abstract representation of the concept. As Marzano et al. (2001) point out, the very act of creating a model of the knowledge enhances student understanding of a concept.

Manipulatives and Student Learning Styles

Research shows that humans better retain that which they do than that which they hear or see. In other words, when students are actively, hands-on engaged with their learning, we can feel confident that they are creating more long-term knowledge and understandings than if they experienced concepts passively. Generally speaking, there are six identified learning styles:

- Auditory: Students with this strength are able to recall what they hear and usually prefer oral instructions. They enjoy talking and interviewing, giving oral reports, and listening to recorded books.

- Visual: Students with this learning style are able to recall what they see and prefer written instructions. They learn by observing and enjoy computer graphics, graphs, charts, diagrams, graphic organizers, and text with many pictures.

- Tactile: Students who are tactile learners learn best by touching. They learn best through the use of manipulatives. They enjoy drawing, making models, and following instructions to make something.

- Kinesthetic: Students with this strength learn by touching or manipulating objects. They need to involve their bodies in learning. They enjoy playing games that involve their whole body, movement activities, making models, and following instructions to make something.

- Global: These learners do not like to be bored. They learn best when information is presented in an interesting manner using attractive materials. Cooperative learning strategies work well with these students. They enjoy computer programs, games, and group activities.

- Analytical: Students with this learning style like to plan and organize their work. They focus on details and are logical. They learn best when goals are clear, requirements are spelled out, and information is presented in sequential steps.

CLASSROOM-TESTED TIP

Good Questioning

Asking questions is an essential part of our approach to teaching and assessing. By asking probing questions, we require students to articulate their thoughts and strategies for solving a problem. Try to include open-ended questions such as these:

- How did you solve it?

- Why did you solve it that way?

- Why do you think you're correct?

- How could you have solved it a different way?

Using manipulatives and other forms of representation appeals to at least five of these learning styles: visual, tactile, kinesthetic, global, and analytical. Visual learners will benefit from seeing and creating models, diagrams, pictures, and other forms of representation as they experience mathematical concepts. Tactile and kinesthetic learners will appreciate touching manipulatives and using them to make models of the mathematical concepts they are learning. Students with a global learning style will enjoy using virtual manipulatives on the computer, participating in group activities that require the use of concrete manipulatives, and being actively engaged as they create their own understandings of math concepts. Finally, analytical learners enjoy planning and organizing their work, so they will apply logic to their use of materials as they work to solve mathematical problems.

As we become more cognizant of the different ways students learn, we can feel confident that by using manipulatives and other representations, we are reaching a majority of our students and tapping into their strengths. Students will be more likely to create lasting understandings of concepts if they learn them in hands-on, active ways.

Manipulatives Can Influence Understanding

In their book *Making Sense*, James Hiebert et al. (1997) argue that the tools students use can result in students constructing different understandings about concepts. Take, for example, fractions and the relationship between the part and the whole. Students who have had many experiences with pattern blocks or Cuisenaire rods have probably already experienced activities dealing with equivalence. For example, most work with pattern blocks will include the relationship of the smaller shapes to the hexagon. How many green triangles does it take to cover the hexagon? Assuming the hexagon is one and it takes six triangles to cover its face, each triangle would be worth one-sixth and if the triangle has a value of one-sixth, what is the value of the red trapezoid? For students to truly understand the relationship of the part to the whole, they need to see how that relationship is changed when the unit changes. What happens to the value of the triangle if the trapezoid is now one? And how would they represent the value of the hexagon? These types of exercises help students understand that fractions are defined in relation to the whole. For this reason, it is important to use a manipulative that allows for different whole units. Fraction circles will not work for an activity such as this because the circle is always the whole. Students can even be challenged to represent the whole as the combination of two of the shapes, as in Figure 2–7. In this case, two hexagons are joined together to make one unit. When this happens, the relationship between the other pattern block shapes changes. Challenge students to continue to represent different units as one and name the other shapes.

The importance of this phenomenon is that teachers must recognize that the tools they select for their students to use will likely affect the understandings they construct. There is no one correct understanding about a concept, so teachers need not be overly concerned with selecting the *right* tool to help develop students' understanding. Rather, they need to be cognizant of the way the tools they choose can influence understandings about a concept, and it would be beneficial to have a conversation with colleagues about this topic when deciding which tools to select.

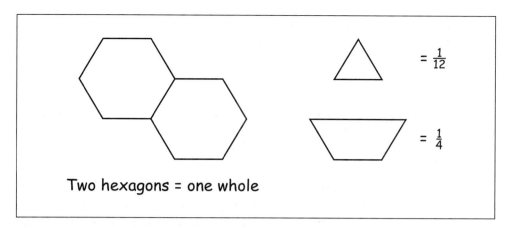

Two hexagons = one whole

Figure 2–7 *Pattern blocks can provide differing units*

Manipulatives and Technology

If you walk into any classroom, you may see many different ways students are using representation to help develop their mathematical understanding. There are manipulatives such as base ten materials or geometric solids, graphic organizers such as Venn diagrams or tables, and more. We see students using technology to represent their thinking. Tools such as virtual manipulatives and interactive white boards are opening up endless possibilities for teachers and students to create meaning about mathematical topics.

Patricia Moyer, Johnna Bolyard, and Mark Spikell, in their article titled, "What Are Virtual Manipulatives?" (2002), establish a definition of virtual manipulatives. They distinguish between "static" and "dynamic" visual representations of concrete manipulatives. Static visual representations are merely pictures on the screen. They resemble concrete manipulatives, but they cannot be acted on in the same way concrete manipulatives can. For example, students may see a picture of two sets of base ten blocks and be asked to add them. With concrete manipulatives, they would be able to combine the two sets, exchanging some blocks for others as necessary, resulting in a sum that was represented by one group of the combined blocks. However, with static visual representations, there is no potential for students to do any manipulating; they are simply looking at a picture, much as they would see in a textbook or on an overhead projector, and they must do the work mentally (or by creating their own representation with blocks or with paper and pencil).

Dynamic visual representations offer teachers and students many of the same opportunities for manipulating as concrete materials do. Students can manipulate polygons or pattern blocks, for example, to illustrate the geometric transformation terms *translation*, *rotation*, and *reflection*. When learning about subtraction with multidigit numbers, students might use a tool, such as a mallet on the virtual manipulative website www.arcytech.org/java/b10blocks, to "break apart" the larger blocks into their smaller components and move them around. The largest online collection of virtual manipulatives can be found at Utah State University's National Library of Virtual Manipulatives at http://nlvm.usu.edu/en/nav/vlibrary.html. This website offers teachers and students learning opportunities in the five NCTM strands: numbers and operations, algebra, geometry, measurement, and data analysis and probability. It includes lesson plans for teachers and ready-made activities for students. One advantage dynamic manipulatives have over concrete materials is that they eliminate the shortage problem we sometimes face when we're teaching a lesson. Online, there is no shortage of blocks or other math tools; students can create a representation using as many pattern blocks as they want without worrying about running out of hexagons, as sometimes happens when we have a class set of manipulatives that we have split into smaller sets for group work.

An interactive white board also offers a different perspective for students when manipulating visual representations. Any virtual manipulative website can be displayed on the large white board, and the dynamic visual representations can be engaged and controlled by the user in a way that is easily visible to peers. For example, when learning about measuring angles, a sixth-grade student can rotate a virtual protractor around an angle to determine its measurement. Geometric or numeric patterns can also be created, analyzed, and completed through the manipulation of the shapes on the board. In Figure 2–8, Mrs. Chatfield uses the interactive board to set up a geometric pattern for students to complete. Interactive white boards have many varied uses and provide us with another way to engage our students and represent concepts in an interesting and active way.

Figure 2–8 *A teacher uses an interactive white board to create a geometric pattern.*

The Role of the Teacher

The teacher's importance when using manipulatives to build understanding cannot be overstated. We are responsible for modeling how to use the manipulatives, asking questions to push understanding, selecting meaningful tasks, and moving students from the concrete to the abstract. It's very important that teachers have a deep understanding of the mathematics they are teaching. How many times have we gone through the motions of teaching a concept without really getting it ourselves? In addition, we need to understand students' thinking, identify misconceptions, and clear up confusions. This can be done only if we thoroughly understand the mathematics we are teaching.

As part of our beginning-of-the-year procedures and throughout the year, we model the behaviors we expect of our students so that they are safe and successful. Using math manipulatives is no exception. If we want our students to use them as tools and not toys, we must allow them first to discover the possibilities of how they might be used in a supervised way. For example, a popular manipulative for learning about geometry, fractions, and other concepts is pattern blocks. These colorful blocks are so appealing to learners, both younger and older, and offer so many possibilities in terms of designing and patterning that we would be mistaken to pass them out to students and jump right into a lesson without giving them exploration time first. Students need time to play, if you will, with the items that they will be using later as learning tools. It's likely many of us know firsthand what happens when we don't conduct a guided discovery of a math tool: The students are so engaged in playing with the manipulatives, or in the mere temptation of playing with them, that we have to continually stop to redirect them just to get through the lesson. By allowing them a few minutes to satisfy their natural curiosity, we are setting our students up for a more meaningful learning experience. Another way to facilitate this exploration is to leave baskets of the manipulatives out and allow students to handle them when they have free time.

Base ten blocks, another popular math manipulative, reinforce the concept that our number system uses a system of ten. However, we cannot assume that children will immediately recognize and understand the relationship between the blocks. In elementary school, base ten blocks are used extensively to model whole-number computation, and students may come with knowledge that a rod is worth ten because it is made of ten unit cubes. At the middle grades level, base ten blocks can also be used to manipulate decimal values, so we may need to assist students in recognizing the relationship of the various shapes when the unit changes. What value does the rod have if the hundreds flat has a value of one? What happens when the thousands cube becomes one? Decimal strips are sometimes used to reinforce the concept of a system of ten, and in fact, middle grades students who find base ten blocks a little babyish may respond better to the use of decimal strips. Because the decimals strips are not three-dimensional, care needs to be taken to ensure students have already conceptualized the relationship of these values. These are just some of the critical roles we play when helping students become proficient in using manipulatives to explore a mathematical concept.

Collecting Math Tools

At the beginning of the year, send a letter home to parents explaining how you use math tools to help their children develop mathematical understandings. Ask them to begin collecting different items that can be incorporated into their children's learning and describe possible uses, such as the following:

- *Craft sticks* can be used to explore the concepts of vertical, horizontal, parallel, perpendicular, right angle, acute angle, obtuse angle, and so on.

- *Beans* can be used to explore volume and capacity or as counters and markers.

- *Egg cartons* can be used to explore addition, subtraction, multiplication, division, and fractions, and they can be cut down to serve as a ten frame.

- *Colorful plastic eggs* can be used to explore addition, subtraction, multiplication, division, and fractions.

- *Small plastic figures*, such as dinosaurs or toy cars, can be used to sort, to explore fractions of a set, or as prompts for creating story problems.

- *Coins* can be used to explore money concepts; plus they're less expensive than buying plastic coins.

- *Small, interesting boxes and containers*, such as cosmetics packaging, can be used to explore the properties of solid figures or the concept of volume, and the numbers on them can be used to create math problems.

- *Everyday containers*, such as milk jugs, soda bottles, and water bottles, can be used to explore volume and capacity and serve as visual benchmarks.

- *Single-serve frozen dinner trays* can be used to hold manipulatives such as number cubes and tiles during a lesson.

- *Plastic sealable bags* of various sizes can be used to hold small sets of manipulatives.

- *Ribbon and yarn* can be used to explore measurement concepts or to create a number line.

- *Wrapping paper* can be used during measurement problem-solving activities or as designs for finding lines of symmetry and creating patterns.

Many of these items can be found around the house, and most parents would be happy to have the opportunity to contribute to their child's instructional program. Invite parents into the classroom to learn ways they can use items at home to support their children's mathematical learning. Middle grades students may not want their parents to continue to be as active in their learning as they were in elementary school, but parent involvement at this level is highly critical. Many parents may begin to back away from helping their students with math at this level due to their own discomfort with the subject. The key here is communication. Keeping parents involved requires keeping them informed. Newsletters that showcase student representations of their work and explanations of the mathematics being studied all will work to keep parents involved.

Questions for Discussion

1. How can "seeing" ideas through the use of manipulatives help students in their growing mathematical understandings?

2. What are some ways we can help students move from the concrete to the abstract? Why is this important?

3. How does the use of manipulatives and other representations appeal to the different learning styles of students?

4. How can the tools we select to use with students influence their understandings about a concept?

5. What is the role of the teacher in using manipulatives to teach mathematics?

3

Using Pictures and Diagrams to Represent Mathematical Thinking

Students who represent the problem in some way are more likely to see important relationships than those who consider the problem without a representation.

—National Council of Teachers of Mathematics,
Principles and Standards for School Mathematics

Pictures and Diagrams

Student use of manipulatives is essential in developing the conceptual understanding of the mathematics at hand, so it isn't an instructional strategy that should be treated lightly. As students move toward more abstract thinking, we need to increase their confidence and abilities in using alternative methods of bringing meaning to their math. With mathematics becoming more complex, students may find the manipulatives are less helpful, and by necessity, they need to rely more on representations that make the problem-solving process more efficient. For this reason, it is important that the representation stage be introduced and modeled while the manipulatives are still on the desk. This allows students an opportunity to make the connection between the two. We must remember that the pictorial representations will have meaning for students only if they have a deep understanding and mastery of the purpose and use of the concrete representations. Research by Piaget confirms the necessity of moving students through these stages, not skipping over them. We need to help students build the bridge between the two. In this chapter, we focus on some specific uses for pictures and diagrams as ways to represent the mathematics and look at how students can use those representations to communicate their solutions.

Moving from Manipulatives to Pictures: Why Transition?

Students in grades 6 through 8 move through several mathematical stages in these three years. They begin refining their skills with whole-number operations and number relationships as they advance to concepts and operations using fractions, decimals, and percentages by the end of sixth grade. Beyond grade 6, integers become a central part of the computational picture, and after that, algebra is the order of the day. Although certain manipulatives may be useful with whole-number operations of manageable size, they become increasingly cumbersome and sometimes downright difficult, if not impossible, to manage with larger and more complex numbers. When working with complex numbers such as decimals, integers, percentages, and/or fractions, students have a choice of trying to make the problem easier by using smaller, more manageable numbers so they can still use the manipulatives. Or they can use some type of pictorial or graphic representation that can be applied to the situation and thereby allow them to represent and solve the problem as it is written. Either method will work. Teachers need to model both processes so that students become proficient in working with complex numbers in problem-solving situations.

The type of representations that students choose can vary widely. For this reason, it is important to allow them the freedom to invent a representation that is meaningful for them. Most middle grades students will not feel the need to draw realistic pictures to help in solving a problem. Because of the nature of the problems and the complexities of the numbers, their representations will be symbolic in nature. Many times, students who initially choose to painstakingly draw representations to help them visualize the problem quickly learn that this method is not time efficient. It's like moving students from Rembrandts to Picassos. Progressing toward more symbolic representations provides students with multiple opportunities to expand their tool kit of strategies when their thinking allows them to make the connections between those symbols and actual shapes.

Fractions 101: Representing Basic Operations

All math teachers have at times struggled with teaching fractional concepts and/or operations, and just as many teachers have been frustrated to the point of raising the white flag in surrender when their students just don't get it, again. Why don't our students seem able to retain fractional concepts from one year to the next or even one day to the next? Does it even matter? How many times in your adult life have you had to explain how to divide fractions or add six 11ths and six 23rds? Let's face it: Fractions hold little or no meaning for our students because they seldom see them or use them in real life, and their only long-term exposure to fractions seems to be in the math classroom. As teachers, we sometimes even struggle to find real-life applications for fractional use beyond dividing a pizza or doubling a recipe! But wait. Before you throw fractions out the window, remember that fractions are not just about adding, subtracting, multiplying, dividing, and don't forget the ever popular "reducing to lowest terms" types of problems. Fractions are found in a multitude of other contexts, such as probability, ratios and proportions, measurement, and later on, scale factor. For this reason, we need to spend additional time helping students internalize fraction concepts and, yes, continue to develop the seemingly elusive number sense as it applies to fractions.

In the middle grades curriculum, little instructional time is devoted to developing the concept of what a fraction is or the meaning behind the computation. After all, there is a lot of curriculum to cover, and those concepts were taught in the earlier grades. Most middle grades students would have little trouble identifying the numerator or denominator of a fraction, and most of them are proficient at identifying the different types of fractions. The problems seem to start when students are asked to apply some of that knowledge to recognizing or creating equivalent fractions, decimals, or percentages. Understanding the relative size of fractions and comparing the values of different representations also present some difficulty for middle grades students. A student who has difficulty comparing fractions, decimals, or percentages to one of the benchmark values such as one-half or who cannot represent values between two specific whole numbers in a variety of ways may not have a solid foundation of the size and relationship of rational numbers. Having students spend a little time demonstrating their knowledge as it relates to different representations of numbers can provide the classroom teacher with a wealth of knowledge about their students' level of mastery in this area.

The student in Figure 3–1 is demonstrating how she would represent values of numbers between the whole numbers seven and eight. As she uses pictorial or numeric representations, she is linking the two. Students can engage in this type of open-ended activity individually or in small groups. Working in small groups, a teacher may not be as confident about an individual student's abilities, but the discussions that take

Figure 3–1 *Representing values between two whole numbers*

place in the group as they complete the task can provide additional insights that may not be evident in an individual's work.

In addition to helping students develop number sense in working with rational numbers, spending a little more time helping them internalize what the computation of those numbers means could lead to long-term retention of the process. There are a number of commercially produced manipulatives that can be used with fraction instruction. Pattern blocks are great for helping students see the relationship of the part to the whole. Using the yellow hexagon as the whole, students can clearly see that the green triangle is one-sixth of the whole, and the red trapezoid is one-half. What happens when the trapezoid becomes the whole? What fraction does the triangle represent now? When the triangle becomes the whole, how do you describe the parallelogram or the hexagon? What happens when one of the other shapes becomes the whole?

As with many other concepts and processes in mathematics, however, fractions are another example of where manipulatives will go only so far. Keep in mind that the goal is to move students toward a more symbolic phase of representation, whether real or invented. It doesn't matter how the representation is drawn as long as it makes the math more meaningful for the student.

What Does a Picture Tell You About the Student's Thinking?

A picture *is* worth a thousand words. Pictorial representations provide a more flexible strategy because students can choose how they want to draw a problem. One distinct advantage in allowing students to choose how they want to represent a problem is the thinking it reveals. That thinking may provide clues that some students are not developmentally where they might need to be or where we think they are in their conceptual understanding of the mathematics. In other words, are they trying to solve fraction problems by picturing the steps in their head, or are they trying to make some sense of the numbers that allows them to understand the math?

The point here is that while students will ultimately need to master the computational algorithm, it is only one strategy, and if we provide our students with only a single strategy for solving computation problems, we are shortchanging them. We need to provide them with classroom experiences that allow them to think about and solve computation problems in a variety of ways. By having students complete pages upon pages of "naked" math computation, you have no sense of their understanding of numbers. Just because students can complete these types of problems does not mean that they can make informed decisions about when to use certain types of computation. Using problems in context and allowing students to choose a representation that demonstrates their understanding of the math will provide much more information than pages of drill.

Consider the following problem:

Represent $\frac{1}{3} + \frac{1}{3} =$ and then show $\frac{1}{3} + \frac{1}{5} =$.

Notice that the question does not ask them to solve the problems but rather to represent their solutions. By having students display some type of pictorial representation for the fraction problems, we can get at any misconceptions a student may have about the numbers and processes themselves.

Most students at this level would have no trouble completing this problem computationally using a traditional algorithm. The fractions are friendly and the computation easy, and we would be none the wiser as to what was really going on inside a student's head. However, if we ask students to represent this problem pictorially, it is possible to see a little of what they are thinking. In this case (see Figure 3–2), Zachary showed what he was thinking about the two problems.

There are a couple of things to look for in Zachary's work. The first key point to note is the representation of the whole. Keep in mind that in working with fractional

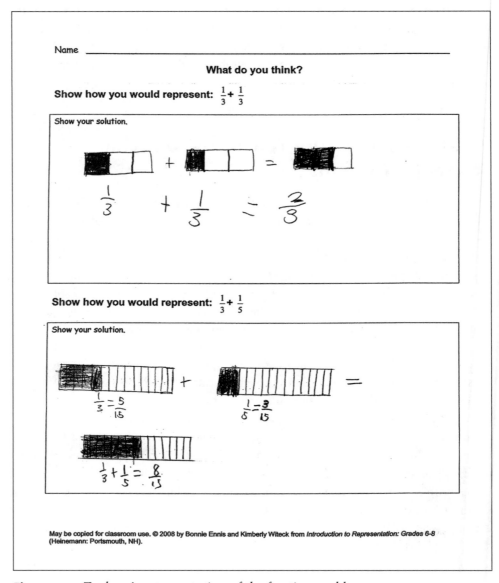

Figure 3–2 *Zachary's representation of the fraction problems*

representations, there are several places where students could demonstrate misconceptions. Fractions only tell us the relationship between the numerator (part) and the denominator (whole). There is nothing to indicate how large or how small the whole is or for that matter the individual pieces. Students need to make some assumptions in drawing these, and this is where you can see if misconceptions exist. In both cases, Zachary apparently was consciously aware of the need to keep the whole the same size as well as the parts. If a student does not have this understanding about size, it may be necessary to use one of the proportional manipulatives available such as Cuisenaire rods.

In the second problem, Zachary represented the equivalent fractions for $\frac{1}{3}$ and $\frac{1}{5}$, but he did so after he found them. Using the equivalent fractions $\frac{5}{15}$ and $\frac{3}{15}$, he then added the two fractions. The fact that he was still making sure that the sections representing one are close in size is important. He obviously didn't use the drawing to solve the problem. For him, the drawing was a way to represent his solution, not a tool in helping him solve the problem.

For some students, the pictorial representation could be used to help them reach a solution. As an example, they might represent the problem $\frac{1}{3} + \frac{1}{5}$ using the method seen in Figure 3–3. A student may choose to first represent the fraction $\frac{1}{3}$ and, using the same grid, proceed to divide the thirds into fifths. If students understand by looking at this representation that each $\frac{1}{3}$ now must have three of the smaller sections, they can shade in those three sections, making sure not to overlap their shading. Their solution now shows that the answer is $\frac{8}{15}$.

In introducing this model to students, it may be seen more clearly if two grids were used and shown as overlapping the other. In this way, students can plainly see how to find the sections to mark off for the second fraction.

This representation works just as well for subtraction. Consider the problem $\frac{7}{8} - \frac{1}{4}$. Students would start with representing the fraction $\frac{7}{8}$ using a grid similar to Figure 3–4. They would then represent the fraction $\frac{1}{4}$ on another grid. By using two separate grids, the students can then overlay the second onto the first and see that if you take $\frac{1}{4}$ from $\frac{7}{8}$ you are left with $\frac{5}{8}$.

Once again, the numbers in these fractions are small, and when problems are presented to students in textbooks, they aren't always this easy. For students struggling with the concept of adding and subtracting fractions with unlike denominators, this visual representation may help bring clarity to the process and allow them to transfer

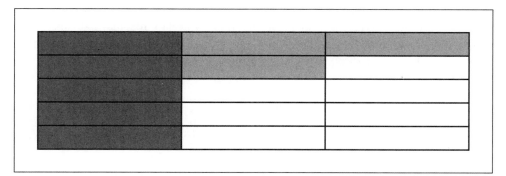

Figure 3–3 *Solution to fraction problem*

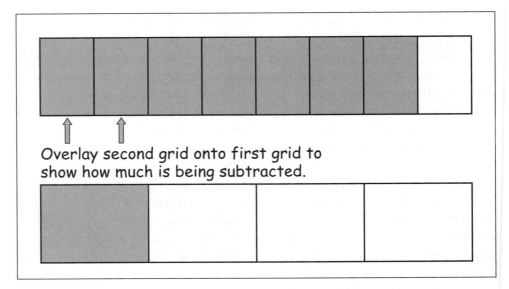

Overlay second grid onto first grid to
show how much is being subtracted.

Figure 3–4 *Pictorial representation for adding fractions*

that information to more complex numbers. By the time students reach middle grades, their required computation with fractions is usually much more advanced. Often, we assume that adding and subtracting proper fractions was taught in fifth grade. It may have been taught, but how well a student retained and understood the concepts may be another story. This strategy of using a representation is a good way to make sure students have a good foundation for more complex problems. Besides, it isn't always a good idea to rush into the purely symbolic method of solving computation problems involving fractions without first making sure students truly understand the concepts. Allowing your students time to represent these problems pictorially can go a long way to having them develop an understanding that is lasting instead of in their head one day and out the next. These strategies work just as well with mixed number computation. Once students have developed proficiency with understanding the representation of proper fractions, moving to work with mixed numbers should follow.

You cannot see your students' thinking without occasionally having them represent problems pictorially. A representation strategy such as this can be used as an exit ticket or warm-up activity that will allow for a quick and easy informal assessment that provides valuable information. Following are some sample exit ticket problems that could be used to get pictorial representations:

1. Margo and Ruth each had identical candy bars. If Margo had $\frac{3}{4}$ of her candy bar left and Ruth had $\frac{1}{2}$ of her candy bar left, how much did they have together?

2. Patty spent $\frac{1}{6}$ of her allowance on a movie ticket and $\frac{1}{4}$ on popcorn. What fraction did she spend?

3. Charlie planted $\frac{2}{5}$ of his garden with beans and $\frac{1}{4}$ with corn. The rest of his garden was planted with tomatoes. What fraction of his garden did he plant with tomatoes?

4. Jason filled his water bottle $\frac{5}{8}$ full. His sister added $\frac{1}{4}$ to the bottle. What fraction of the bottle is empty?

5. Kurt bought a bag of peanuts at the ballgame. He ate $\frac{1}{3}$ of the peanuts in the bag, and his brother Ryan ate $\frac{2}{5}$ of the peanuts. How much of the bag of peanuts remained uneaten?

C L A S S R O O M - T E S T E D   T I P

Exit tickets are great ways of assessing students' understanding of the daily lesson. By asking students to represent problems just before exiting the classroom and collecting their papers as they leave, you have a reliable method of assessment that can be used to inform the next day's instruction. These can also be used as warm-ups in the same way if you have your students complete them at the beginning of class. Having them do a quick check at the start of class provides you with some instant data on how students are progressing with a particular skill or concept. By doing this at the start of class, you can quickly look over their work and make decisions for that day's lesson or flexible grouping time.

The same type of thinking can be assessed when looking at multiplication and division of fractions. If you ask any adult if they can show a pictorial representation of $\frac{2}{5} \times \frac{1}{4}$ or $\frac{2}{5} \div \frac{1}{4}$, they would be hard pressed to illustrate a satisfactory representation of why the computation works. They would have no trouble giving you an answer, but could they show a representation that underscored their understanding of what the problem meant? Multiplying and dividing fractions are two of those processes that are easier done than justified. The same holds true for teaching the concepts. Rushing to the algorithm because it is "easier" to teach and learn almost always shortchanges a student's chances of being able to construct meaning about why the problem is solved in that manner. Most textbooks at this level will present the algorithm first and very little about the representation of the problems. There may be a few contextual problems, but most are presented in isolation. How many of us have heard the rule, "just multiply the numerators and then multiply the denominators?" Why is it that when you multiply fractions the answer gets smaller, and just the opposite happens with whole numbers? As students learn new concepts, they will keep trying to bring in prior knowledge that will help them understand the new knowledge. In this case, whole-number rules about the value of the answers are exactly the opposite when it comes to multiplying and dividing fractions. When representing multiplication of fraction problems, the language that needs to be reinforced over and over again is that the multiplication symbol should be read "of." This may help students understand why the answers become smaller when you are multiplying.

When representing multiplication of fractions, manipulatives are helpful; counters could be used as well as pattern blocks and Cuisenaire rods. The manipulatives are useful especially when the problem doesn't require further division of the unit. If you start with a problem such as $\frac{1}{3} \times 3$, then the unit does not require any division, and a student can easily see how to take $\frac{1}{3}$ of the units. (See Figure 3–5.) Most textbooks present multiplication of proper fractions and whole numbers first for this reason. As a precursor to multiplying proper fractions and later mixed numbers, this is a good way to transition.

Multiplying proper fractions and mixed numbers becomes more challenging, and students may not see that when you are starting with a part and then taking a part of that, the answer is less in value. Students will still try to apply whole-number relationships here, and they may still want to think of multiplying fractions as repeated addition. For that reason, representations are important. They may not be as easily created without some basic understanding of what is taking place in the problem. One method that works well with friendly numbers is paper folding. Students multiplying $\frac{1}{3} \times \frac{1}{5}$ would first fold their paper in one direction in fifths and then rotate the paper to fold it in the other direction in thirds. (See Figure 3–6.) Starting with paper folding reinforces the idea of folding in a different direction instead of dividing the already divided sections further. It is essential at this point to read the problem as $\frac{1}{3}$ of $\frac{1}{5}$ to reinforce the idea of multiplication of fractions as taking part of a part.

By doing this paper folding activity, students can first see the unit divided into fifths with one-fifth shaded. With the folded thirds, you can see that by taking $\frac{1}{3}$ of one-fifth, you actually end up with $\frac{1}{15}$. With this visual, the students can see that nothing is added to the unit, and in this case, the sections get smaller and you are taking fewer of them, so the answer will be a smaller value.

The same type of representation can be done using two-color counters, or in the absence of counters, students can represent the problem by drawing circles and shading in the parts; it is a little more cumbersome, but it is an effective tool for understanding why the unit must be subdivided. Mrs. Hartley was using counters as a way of introducing this process to her sixth-grade class. Each student was given a bag of two-color counters, a recording sheet, and a two-color pencil. She wrote the problem $\frac{2}{3} \times \frac{2}{3}$ on the board and asked her students what they thought it meant. Jane raised her

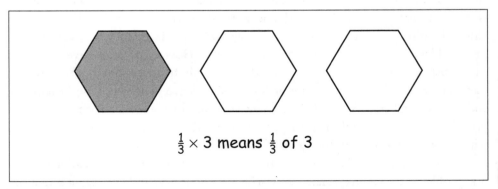

$\frac{1}{3} \times 3$ means $\frac{1}{3}$ of 3

Figure 3–5 *Pattern blocks can be used to model multiplication of fractions and whole numbers.*

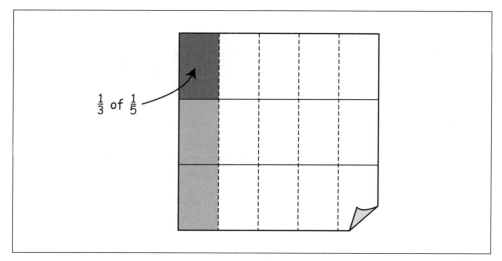

Figure 3–6 *Using paper folding to model multiplication of proper fractions*

hand and offered, "I think it might mean you take three groups of $\frac{1}{5}$, but I'm not sure since you can turn multiplication problems around when you multiply; it might be five groups of $\frac{1}{3}$." Susan raised her hand to add, "I don't think that can be true since you read the multiplication symbol as 'of,' and that means that the answer has to be smaller than both $\frac{2}{3}$ and $\frac{2}{5}$."

Mrs. Hartley asked them to start by representing $\frac{2}{5}$, which meant the students used five counters and turned only two of them to the opposite color. She asked them to look only at the two counters that represented $\frac{2}{5}$ because the problem said to take $\frac{2}{3}$ of $\frac{2}{5}$, not $\frac{5}{5}$. She next asked them, "Can you put those two counters into equal groups of three to represent the thirds?" There weren't any positive responses, and she asked if any of them had ideas on how they could proceed since they couldn't divide these two counters further.

Jeff raised his hand to ask, "How can we ever divide two pieces evenly into three? Don't we need more pieces?" Marcus raised his hand and asked, "Can't we get more pieces if we make another fraction that is equivalent to $\frac{2}{5}$?" With heads nodding, everyone pulled out more counters and proceeded to find another fraction that was equivalent to $\frac{2}{5}$ but could be divided into thirds.

Marcus came up with the possible solution first. His equivalent fraction for $\frac{2}{5}$ was $\frac{6}{15}$, and since he knew he could divide six into three equal sections, he knew he was on the right track. See Figure 3–7 for Marcus's solution.

Marcus had the right idea, but he still wasn't sure how to interpret what he had in front of him. He pulled out the six counters that represented the part he needed to divide into thirds and placed them in thirds. Each third had two counters, and from here, he was able to determine that $\frac{2}{3}$ would be four counters. He began to describe his solution to the class, "I know that $\frac{6}{15}$ is equivalent to $\frac{2}{5}$, and so I took the six counters out and put them in three groups of two each. Since the problem said to take $\frac{2}{3}$, I grouped two of those groups to get four counters. I know my answer can't be four, so it must be a numerator, but I don't know what the denominator is."

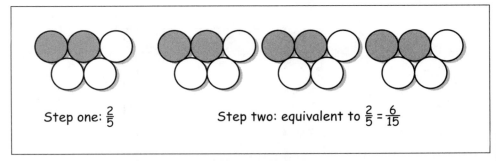

Figure 3–7 *Marcus's solution using two-color counters*

Jeff was able to offer that since the fraction was $\frac{6}{15}$, 15 must be the denominator and the answer had to be $\frac{4}{15}$.

Both of these methods work for helping students understand and represent what is happening in the multiplication of fractions. Allow student opportunities to explore these models before they learn the algorithm and by all means allow time for reflection on the answers. It isn't likely students will take the time to look for meaning once they know how to multiply fractions.

Ours is not to wonder why. Just invert and multiply.

Making sense of dividing fractions is much more difficult than memorizing the rules for how to solve them. Here again, how many of us can create a visual representation for the following problem: $18 \div \frac{3}{4}$? Out of context, the problem becomes more difficult, and for the middle grades student trying to transfer whole-number rules to the division of fractions, it can be almost impossible to understand why the answer is 24. One way of representing this problem is to take eighteen sheets of paper, fold each of them into fourths, and count how many groups of $\frac{3}{4}$ you get. Obviously, students aren't going to be able to divide paper all of the time, so it is important to show them the context relationship of the division problem. Helping them make that connection should ensure their understanding of what happens when you divide fractions.

Students need to have an understanding of what division means and how that meaning relates to the different types of division problems they are going to see. Not all division problems are created equal! (See Figure 3–8.)

Problem	What does it mean?
$3 \div 2$	2-foot pieces cut from a 3-foot rope
$3 \div \frac{1}{2}$	$\frac{1}{2}$-foot pieces cut from a 3-foot rope
$3\frac{1}{4} \div \frac{1}{2}$	$\frac{1}{2}$-foot pieces cut from a $3\frac{1}{4}$-foot rope
$\frac{1}{2} \div 3$	3-foot pieces cut from a $\frac{1}{2}$-foot rope *
	*While you do get a fractional quotient, the interpretation of the answer is zero.

Figure 3–8 *Examples of different types of division problems using fractions*

Mrs. Townsend gave her seventh-grade class the following task to solve:

Mrs. Townsend is making poodle skirts for the 50s rock-and-roll show. She purchased 12 yards of fabric. If each skirt requires $\frac{7}{8}$ yard of fabric, how many skirts can she make?

Because she was looking for students to reflect on their work and show that they understood the algorithm they were solving, she asked them draw a picture that could be used to explain the process. Jessica started by drawing a large rectangle on her paper to represent the 12 yards of fabric. She then divided the fabric into 12 sections. When she was questioned as to why she divided the fabric in this manner, she replied, "I know that $\frac{7}{8}$ is almost a whole yard, so I can at least get 12 skirts from the fabric if I divide it into 12 sections. Then I can take the $\frac{7}{8}$ from each section and combine the remaining $\frac{1}{8}$ pieces to see how many more groups of $\frac{7}{8}$ I have." Jessica's solution is seen in Figure 3–9.

When Jessica completed her picture, she shared that her answer was 13 skirts with $\frac{5}{8}$ remaining. She then proceeded to verify her results by dividing $12 \div \frac{7}{8}$. She changed the division sign to a multiplication sign and inverted the fraction to $\frac{8}{7}$. Her computation showed $\frac{96}{7}$, which she converted to $13\frac{5}{7}$. She gave her work a puzzled look and knew something wasn't right. How can her diagram show the answer as 13 with $\frac{5}{8}$ remaining and her computation show $13\frac{5}{7}$? What Jessica failed to realize is that both of her answers were correct. The error was in her interpretation of the numbers. When her computation resulted in $13\frac{5}{7}$, it should have been interpreted as 13 skirts and $\frac{5}{7}$ of another one. When you take $\frac{5}{7}$ of $\frac{7}{8}$ you end up with $\frac{5}{8}$, so both of her solutions were correct.

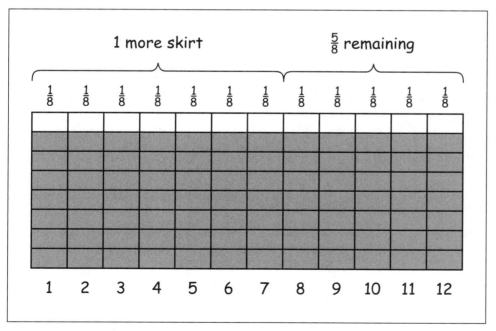

Figure 3–9 *Jessica's representation of the poodle skirt problem*

If students are unable to describe what the problems mean either in words, symbols, or pictures, how can their numeric answers be checked for reasonableness? Students have little number sense when they have to rely solely on numeric solutions. This is especially true when it comes to fractions. As much as possible, put the problems in context and require some type of pictorial representation or student reflection.

The following problems can be used as exit tickets, warm-ups, or check-ups.

1. If you have $2\frac{3}{4}$ pounds of ground beef, how many $\frac{1}{4}$-pound hamburgers can you make?

2. How many 9-inch pieces of rope can be cut from $1\frac{1}{2}$ yards of rope?

3. Marita has $2\frac{1}{4}$ gallons of orange juice concentrate. It takes $\frac{3}{4}$ gallon to make a pitcher of orange juice. How many pitchers can she make?

Take Your Cue from Reading Instruction

If you look in any good reading manual, you will see a great deal of importance is placed on getting students ready to read. Building background knowledge is one of the key components in reading instruction. Its purpose is to increase the likelihood that a student will not only be interested in but also will understand what he or she is about to read. It is no different with math, especially in the use of fractions. In the foreword of the book *Fractions, Decimals, Ratios and Percents* (Barnett, Goldenstein, and Jackson 1994), Judith and Lee Shulman write, "Veteran teachers understand that when students leave behind the safe harbor of operations on whole numbers and enter the abyss of fractions, decimals, ratios, and percents, problems ensue (stuff happens)." We need to actively build on what students already know and can do with whole-number computation. Regardless of the grade level and content, activating prior knowledge is essential to bringing meaning to new concepts. Brain research indicates that when new information is introduced, students are trying to connect it with what they already know. Isn't that how we all approach new knowledge? Many students do not see math around them on a daily basis, and unlike reading, they seldom go home at night and solve math problems for pleasure. They don't realize how math impacts their lives, so it becomes important for us to find ways to make the math meaningful to them and connect it to their world.

Before: Activate Prior Knowledge

Jump-start your students' thinking. Fractions are not just about pizza and dividing rectangles, and yet most of us learned fractions in that context. Before starting instruction on a new concept or skill, take the time to find out what the students already know about fractions and how they think about them. One way to do this is to engage students in a freewriting activity. It is more like a freewriting and drawing activity, but it allows students to demonstrate their understandings or misunderstandings where fractions are concerned. Students in Mrs. Harbinson's seventh-grade class regularly engage in writing activities prior to learning new concepts and skills. Before the unit on fractions, she had them begin with a blank sheet of paper and asked them to represent or describe as many fractional concepts and operations with fractions as they could. By encouraging them to use not only words and numbers but also pictures and diagrams, she was able to see how some of them visualized the concepts. Seeing students use nonlinguistic forms of representations to illustrate fractional terms and processes can be very insightful for a classroom teacher.

During: On to the New Material

If you look in almost any mathematics textbook at this level, you will surely find problems requiring students to put four or five fractions in order from smallest to greatest. What strategy do we use? Most textbooks will provide examples where students are asked to find common denominators for all of the fractions before putting them in order. Computationally, this makes the end result easier to determine, but what does it tell us about the students' abilities to understand the magnitude of the numbers? Keep in mind, if the purpose of putting fractions in order of smallest to greatest is to assess student understanding of the size of a given fraction and its relationship to other fractions, can we assess that accurately if we provide them with a computation model that they only have to replicate over and over again? Give students two whole numbers and ask them to represent as many different values as they can for numbers that fall between these two numbers.

After: Been There, Done That—Moving On!

Don't you just love it when students say, "Why are we doing this? We learned that in the last chapter," and "We've already taken the test," or "Why are we doing a geometry problem when we are supposed to be working on division?" Like it or not, that is how most students view mathematics instruction: in isolation. It becomes imperative to continue to spiral back and reassess student thinking as well as help students make connections to the new concepts as we are teaching them. We need to provide students with opportunities to demonstrate the connective nature of the mathematics and extend and refine their thinking as it relates to the more complex processes.

As an example, students can use the same number line used for ordering fractions to order decimals and then order decimals and fractions in combination. Base ten blocks and their appropriate representations can now be used to support instruction using decimals. If the one thousand cube now becomes one unit, what does the ten rod become? Decimals, fractions, and percentages are often found in isolation in many textbooks. Why not combine the representations to help students make the connection?

Using decimal squares, you can ask students if the figure represents $\frac{3}{10}$, 30 percent, or .3. Ask students how many different ways they can represent a certain number or how many names they can find for a certain representation. All of these activities lead to an increase in number sense and an understanding of the connected nature of the mathematics.

The Role of the Teacher

It is important for teachers to provide students with multiple opportunities to interact with concepts and express themselves mathematically so that their thinking is revealed. It doesn't come from pages of drill and kill, and it doesn't come from limiting them to one numeric representation. Studies such as TIMSS (Trends in International Mathematics and Science Study) illustrate the need for a change in our approach to mathematics instruction. One such change is in allowing students to work through problem-solving situations either independently or cooperatively and construct meaning from the mathematics without having to be told what math is involved. Students who are allowed to work through problems without first having to memorize steps in an algorithm are much more likely to internalize the mathematics and thus reduce the nearly 53 percent of time spent reviewing concepts in an average eighth-grade classroom (Hiebert et al. 2003).

A mathematics class rich in context and problem-solving opportunities is much more likely to yield students ready for more complex situations, and allowing students to use their own representations to illustrate their thinking will help teachers immediately zero in on misconceptions and inefficient strategies.

The Role of Technology

Getting middle grades students to eagerly create and share their representations is not an easy task. Many students at this level are not comfortable sharing their thinking with the rest of the class. Technologies such as document cameras and smart boards provide a venue for sharing information that is new and somewhat interesting for middle grades students. Given a problem to solve, groups of students can now easily share their discoveries and show the rest of the class the computations and diagrams they used in the solution. The document camera is a wonderful tool to use with this strategy. Gone is the need for creating a transparency of student work for the next day's presentation or having students work out their problems on large sheets of chart paper. The document camera allows students to display their work immediately and save it for later use if needed. "Integrating the simple technology of a document camera blurs the line between teachers and learners. As students learn from each other . . . " (Small and Anderson 2007).

In Figure 3–10, a student shares his group's method for solving a problem with the rest of the class. The cameras provide a powerful tool for facilitating and encouraging discussions and facilitate the sharing of student work.

Smart board technology gives students a magic way of manipulating shapes, numbers, patterns, and graphs. With the appropriate software, a plain white board can be an engaging tool that motivates students to share their thinking. Math classrooms need to be engaging. Our students are growing up in a video world where, with the click of a mouse or movement of a joystick, they can manipulate just about anything on a video screen. By giving them some of the same technology in the math classroom, not only are they going to be motivated to stay engaged, but they are also much likelier to willingly share their information with others.

Figure 3–10 *A document camera provides a tool for sharing student work.*

Questions for Discussion

1. How can a standards-based classroom be a problem-based classroom?

2. How can the use of representations help students extend and refine their understanding of the mathematics?

3. What connections to the context can students demonstrate with their representations?

4. How can teachers use alternative forms of representations to help jump-start instruction?

5. How can technology facilitate the sharing of student representations?

4

Using Numbers and Symbols to Represent Mathematical Ideas

Like other forms of written literacy, mathematical representations allow for visual inspection of work and reduce cognitive demands on memory.

—Sara P. Fisher and Christopher Hartmann, "Math through the Mind's Eye"

Moving from Pictures to Equations

As we discussed in Chapter 3, pictures are an important way students learn to show their mathematical thinking, and the sophistication of their pictorial representations grows developmentally. The leap from pictures to numbers and symbols, however, is not an easy one for some students. Moving from the concrete to the abstract requires a deep understanding of a concept, although we might argue that there are plenty of students who can use numbers successfully without having worked in the concrete first. When we ask students to explain their thinking in words, or even to go from the abstract of numbers to creating a concrete model of the process they used, we find that there are holes in their understanding. They are often performing certain procedures automatically without a foundation of real understanding about why those procedures work or what they mean. A fractional operation is a good example of this. Our goal is to move students from pictures to equations when they are developmentally ready and to guide them toward more standard numeric representations when appropriate. Early work in the area of algebra starts with finding the unknown in a basic number sentence. As students progress to middle grades, the complexity of the problems and numbers increases. Consider the following problem given to an eighth-grade group of students:

Together, a mango and a pineapple weigh 1.5 pounds. A mango and an apple weigh 1.75 pounds together, and the apple and the pineapple weigh 1.8 pounds. How much does each piece of fruit weigh?

Students will approach this problem in one of two ways. They will either add up all of the weights without taking time to see if they answered the question that was asked, or if they are trying to apply algebra rules, they will start assigning xs and ys to the unknowns. In this case, the teacher, Mr. Dunn, wanted his students to use a combination of strategies. He wanted them to use some type of manipulative to model the problem, but he also wanted the manipulative to be translated to symbols and numbers. Thus, he gave the students a variety of tools for solving the problem. He gave them a calculator, three different colors of tiles to represent the fruit, and a picture of a balance scale. Understanding the power of the equal sign in an equation is sometimes difficult for students, and equating it with a balance scale helps to reinforce the purpose and use of the equal sign. He also gave them sheets of chart paper to show the progression of the solutions.

Mark's group started in right away, and with Mr. Dunn's permission, they wrote letters on top of the number tiles so they could remember which color was used for which fruit. The red tile represented the apple, so it received an A at the top; the yellow tile stood for the pineapple, so they put a P at the top; and the orange tile stood for the mango, so M was put at the top. With the tiles labeled, the group began writing down in a table what they knew and translating the facts into equations. Their chart is seen in Figure 4–1.

As Mark's group prepares their chart, they notice that individually the equations do not provide them with a way to solve the problem, so at first, they think they need to use the guess-and-check method. They reason that perhaps they could come up with the numbers that would fit in all three equations by just trying a lot of different numbers. Sara decides that they could be doing that all day because they aren't just working with whole numbers. Lee then suggests they combine the first two equations so that they have: $m + p + m + a = 3.25$ pounds. Sara sees right away that there are two places where m is found in the equation, and she knows she can combine like terms, so she writes: $2m + p + a = 3.25$ pounds. They still aren't sure if they are on the right track, but Mark suggests substituting 1.8 for the $p + a$ in the equation since they already know that $p + a = 1.8$ pounds. The equation now reads: $2m + 1.8 = 3.25$. With his calculator, Mark subtracts 1.8 from 3.25 and gets 1.45, so he writes $2m = 1.45$, which means m must equal 0.725. With information about the value of m, Mark's

Known Information	Equations
mango and pineapple weigh 1.5 pounds	$m + p = 1.5$ pounds
mango and apple weigh 1.75 pounds	$m + a = 1.75$ pounds
apple and pineapple weigh 1.8 pounds	$a + p = 1.8$ pounds

Figure 4–1 *Representation of the fruit problem*

group sets out to rewrite the equations with the new information. They come up with, $0.725 + p = 1.5$ and $0.725 + a = 1.75$. Lee doesn't think they can rewrite the equation for apple + pineapple until they solve one of the first two equations, since they don't have information about a or p.

Sara solves the first equation by subtracting 0.725 from 1.5 to get $p = 0.775$, and Mark solves the second equation to get $a = 1.025$. Since they now know the values of a and p, they need to substitute both as a check. Because $0.775 + 1.025 = 1.8$, they now know they have a correct solution for each of the variables. This wasn't an easy problem, but the context was reasonable, so the variables made sense and the numbers were small and manageable. With calculators in hand, the group was able to focus on the procedures for finding each value instead of spending time doing the subtraction and division.

In this chapter, we discuss the importance of developing students' understanding of what numbers and symbols mean and ways we can support them in this growth. We also discuss the role of invented algorithms and the use of equations to solve problems and visualize math ideas. Finally, the role of the teacher in this area of student learning is examined.

It's All About Timing

Timing is everything, as they say. If we attempt to move our students from the concrete to the abstract too early, or worse yet, skip the concrete altogether, we'll find ourselves with a group of students who are consumed with remembering formulas and procedures without really thinking about the mathematics behind a problem. If they can't recall those algorithms, they'll have absolutely nothing to fall back on. We do a disservice to students when we teach procedures rather than concepts. How many of us learned that the formula for the area of a rectangle is length times width? It's likely that we stored this procedural approach to an area of our brain and retrieved it when we thought it was applicable without creating a visual in our head or on paper that would assist in our understanding of the problem. Similarly, we may have the formula for the perimeter of a rectangle tucked safely away: $2s^1 + 2s^2$. How many times, though, have we seen students faced with a perimeter problem of an irregular polygon who did not use the understanding that perimeter is the distance *around* something? Rather, they tried to apply the formula for a rectangle to the irregular polygon and froze up when they could not make it work. The student had nothing to fall back on—no mental toolbox from which to pull different strategies.

What do numbers really mean? How can we support students' growing understanding of numbers and symbols? These are important questions that we must ask ourselves as we plan meaningful learning experiences for our students. Defining the word *number* is not an easy task in itself. Indeed, one Web inquiry into the definition of the word led us to more than ten separate definitions. It is no wonder that without concrete learning experiences, some students find conventions such as numbers and symbols very difficult to master.

One way we can help our students to make the connection between the concrete and the abstract is by using manipulatives or models, linking the process to numbers and symbols, and then weaning them from the manipulatives. Integers provide another example of where it is important to hold students accountable for developing conceptual knowledge. Like fractions, the procedures for operations with integers are sometimes easier to teach and learn than understand. Many students can remember the rules for adding, subtracting, multiplying, and dividing integers and may not have any trouble completing a page of computation, but when asked to explain why their answer is correct, how many of them could illustrate or justify their response? It is important to use models that will help students develop that understanding of why the rules work and then transition to some type of symbolic representation that will allow them practice in applying the rules.

It is difficult, but not impossible, to show students representations of negative numbers. Most middle grades students can already make the connection to the idea of loss of yardage in a football game or money concepts related to credits and debits; however, they may not realize that they are dealing with negative numbers when discussing above sea level and below sea level measurements. Once students have made this connection, the next step is to introduce a model that can be used to manipulate the various problems. One of the more frequently used models when working with integers is the two-color counter. These counters can be used to represent positive with one color (most often white or yellow) and negative with the other (red). Many textbooks are using this representation more and more as they introduce concepts and operations with integers. As students begin work with integers, it is important to begin by developing the concept of zero as it relates to one positive and one negative.

When introducing operations with integers, Mr. Briggs first works to help students understand the model for zero, and since his students are already familiar with the idea of gains and losses in a football game, he plans to use the context of football. Displayed on the interactive white board as the students entered the room is a football field with one football on the 50-yard line. Combining interactive technology and a sport is a sure way to generate excitement, even in seventh-grade students. Dante immediately wanted to know where the players were and what they would call their team.

Mr. Briggs explained that they were going to begin looking at adding integers today, and they were going to look at how adding integers related to playing football. He then gave each student their own scorecard, divided the class into two teams, and explained to them how to record their scores on the scorecard. Since they had already been working with integers, they were familiar with the notation that went along with negatives and positives. He then told them to record a play that ended closer to their goal as a positive number and a play that resulted in a loss of yardage as a negative. For example, he said, "If you start at the 50-yard line and your ball ends up at the 45-yard line on your side of the field, it would be recorded as a +5 yards. If it ends at the 45-yard line closest to your opponent, it would be recorded as −5." A series will consist of four plays at which time each member of the team needs to record their net result. In other words, how many yards did the team gain or lose altogether?

He explained that each play would be determined by a card drawn from a stack of regular playing cards. If he drew a red 5, that meant a loss of 5 yards, but if he

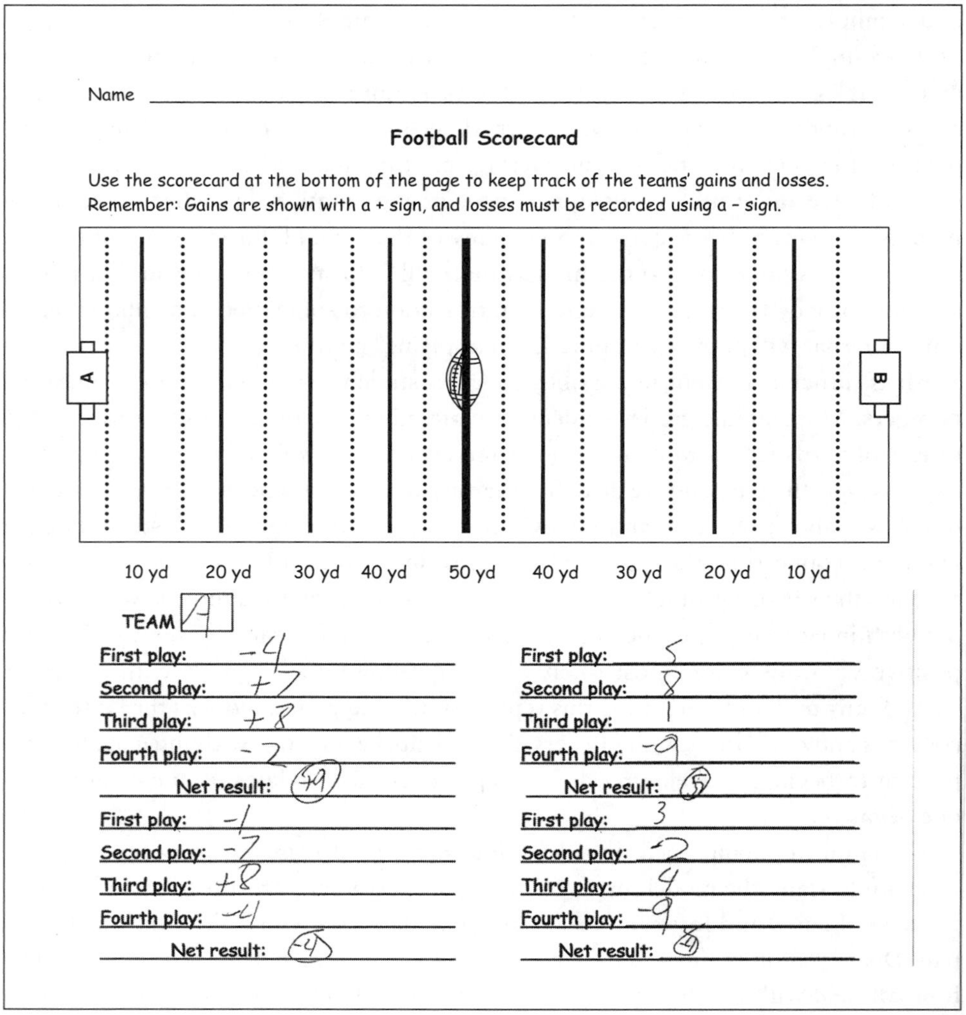
Name

Football Scorecard

Use the scorecard at the bottom of the page to keep track of the teams' gains and losses.
Remember: Gains are shown with a + sign, and losses must be recorded using a – sign.

TEAM A

First play:	–4	First play:	5
Second play:	+7	Second play:	8
Third play:	+8	Third play:	1
Fourth play:	–2	Fourth play:	–9
Net result:	+9	Net result:	5
First play:	–1	First play:	3
Second play:	–7	Second play:	–2
Third play:	+8	Third play:	4
Fourth play:	–4	Fourth play:	–9
Net result:	–4	Net result:	4

Figure 4–2 *Complete chart of the football game*

drew a black 4, it was a gain of 4 yards. Using the deck of cards with the jacks, queens, and kings removed, he was reinforcing the idea of seeing positive and negatives as two different colors. When the two-color counters were used, they would already be accustomed to seeing positive and negative in terms of colors. He took them through one complete series of plays to model the process, and then he let the groups work on their own. This type of activity illustrates how context can help students understand and draw meaning from computations that may otherwise be difficult. Figure 4–2 shows how Shawn's group completed the series of problems.

The Role of Alternative Algorithms

Alternative, or invented, algorithms are procedures students have invented to help them solve mathematical problems. They are termed *alternative* because they are often idiosyncratic and do not resemble the algorithms that are traditionally associated with

Helping students gain flexibility and fluency in mathematical thinking should be one of the goals of any math program. There are many ways we can help students to develop these skills. Try these activities as warm-ups, sponges, or homework assignments.

- Renaming a Number: Help students to think about different ways we can name numbers. For example: 112 = 100 + 12 or 50 + 50 + 10 + 2. A wonderful game for helping students develop fluency with computation and flexibility with numbers is the commercially available 24 Game. It is a mental game that requires students to combine four numbers in such a way that they end up with a total of twenty-four.

- Target Number: This activity is similar to renaming a number. You select a target number, and students must think of as many possible ways to reach the target number as they can. For example, 12 can be reached by dividing 144 by 12 or by doubling 6.

- Who Am I? Students are given clues about numbers and must guess the number. For example, "I am an odd number that is a multiple of three and I am between sixteen and twenty-five" (twenty-one). Students can generate their own "Who Am I?" riddles.

- Buzz: Students gather in a circle. A number is selected, such as six, and as the students count starting at one, those students who would say a multiple of six instead say, "Buzz."

- Predict Then Count: The group gathers in a circle and counts off by ones. The leader then selects a value to count by (such as one-half), and before counting, students can predict what they think will be the last number announced. For example, if there are nineteen children in the class and they are counting by one-half each time, students might predict that ten will be the last number announced, or some may correctly predict that nine and one-half will be the last number. After counting, discuss how the predictions compared with the actual number and solicit strategies for how students figured it out.

- What's the Question? Give students an answer such as, "The answer is fifty. What's the question?" Student responses might be, "How much is two quarters [or half a dollar]?" or "How many pounds does my seven-year-old brother weigh?" and so on.

- Starting Where? Ask students to count by five, for example, and they respond by asking you, "Starting where?" Choose different numbers to start with, such as "Count by fives starting at nineteen." Get them to count over landmark numbers, such as one hundred, to build their fluency with larger numbers as well.

operations. *Principles and Standards for School Mathematics* (NCTM 2000) asserts the importance of encouraging students to use written mathematical representations to help them make sense, even if those representations are unconventional. Division lends itself to the creation of alternative algorithms. Traditionally, students are taught to divide, multiply, subtract, compare, and bring down when doing long division, and they may have even created a mnemonic device for helping them to remember those steps. For students relying strictly on the traditional method of solving division with little to no understanding of why the computations work, division becomes something to be relearned year after year. Some students, though, will find ways to divide larger numbers without having to follow the traditional procedure.

There are two ways to think about division problems. The first way is usually called the fair share method. An example of a fair share problem would be: Jeffery has 588 sports cards and 12 albums. If he wants an equal amount in each album, how many cards will he put in each album? In solving this problem, a student may choose to represent the problem using base ten blocks and start with the 588, sharing out each quantity among 12 different areas. This of course requires some trading of units, but students practicing the idea of fair share using base ten generally gain a sense of the numbers in terms of value instead of digits.

The other type of division problem can be thought of as a measurement or repeated subtraction problem. Consider the following problem.

The farmers' market has 750 pears to put in boxes. If each box holds 25 pears, how many boxes will they need?

Figure 4–3 *Base ten blocks can be used to represent fair share division*

In solving a problem such as this, students may use the grab method, where they take out multiples of the divisor from the dividend and then on the side indicate how many groups (or "grabs") of the divisor are taken out. As they take out the multiples, they continue to subtract from the dividend until they cannot take any more, leaving a remainder. They then add up the grabs, giving them the quotient with remainder. As students experiment with this approach to division, they soon learn that it doesn't matter what multiples they use first; eventually, if they keep grabbing out multiples of the divisor, they will get the same quotient. That is, one student may keep grabbing out fifty or one hundred because that is an easy number for them to work with. Eventually, they will subtract the multiple out enough times, and then they will add up their grabs and arrive at the same quotient. (See Figure 4–4.) Again, this strategy for solving division problems is one that is developed *first* through the use of manipulatives and then linked to the symbolic representation.

The wonderful thing about alternative algorithms is that they develop out of a student's growing understanding of a concept, without having conventions and rules applied to them. These invented approaches to solving problems provide us, their teachers, with great insight into their understanding of a concept, their confidence as mathematicians, and their development as independent thinkers. It is so exciting to see a student solve a problem in a way we never thought of. We need to encourage our students to solve mathematical problems in a way that makes sense to them so that they are thinking and reasoning about numbers. A student who solves multiplication problems only through repeated addition and counting or by drawing a picture may need to be exposed to and guided toward more efficient strategies. That is not to say that we should dismiss their approach to solving a problem, but rather, through exposing them to and discussing the way other students solve problems, we can coach them to the next level.

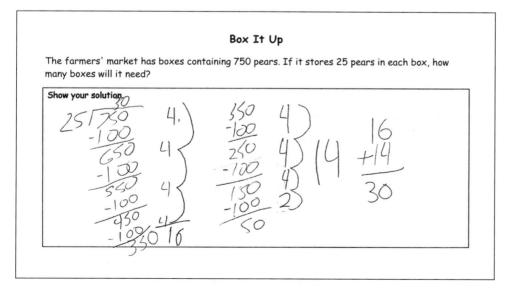

Figure 4–4 *An alternative representation for division*

Using Equations to Solve Problems and Visualize Ideas

As mentioned earlier, we do a great disservice to our students when we teach procedures and algorithms without letting them develop their own understanding of a concept. However, we would be negligent as well if we did not help students make the connection between ideas and equations and see how equations can help us solve problems and visualize ideas.

An equation represents a whole idea such as $\frac{1}{4} + \frac{1}{2} = \frac{3}{4}$. For any equation to have meaning for students, other than as a memorized fact, they must understand several things. First, they have to understand what $\frac{1}{4}, \frac{1}{2}$, and $\frac{3}{4}$ mean (they represent different size parts of a whole), and perhaps more important, they must understand what the equal sign represents. The notion that the equal sign balances an equation is essential. Here is one experience a teacher had when assessing her students' understanding of this concept:

Mrs. Fowle: I am going to write an equation on the board, and I want you to give me your thoughts. [She writes $15 = n + 7$.]

Maria: You can't write it like that.

Mrs. Fowle: No? Why not?

Maria: Because the answer has to come last, and fifteen is the answer.

Mrs. Fowle: OK. What does this symbol mean [pointing to the equal sign]?

Brad: It means the answer. Like, if I had the problem three times six equals eighteen, the equal sign tells you that the answer is next, which is eighteen.

Mrs. Fowle: Does anyone else have any thoughts?

Aidan: I think the answer can come first because you can add something to seven that equals fifteen, so what you're really saying is fifteen equals fifteen.

Mrs. Fowle: It sounds like Aidan has noticed something about what's on each side of the equal sign. Let's look at this equation. [She writes $3 \times 4 = 4 \times 3$ on the board.]

Chris: Well, three times four equals twelve, and four times three equals twelve, so both sides equal the same thing.

Mrs. Fowle: Let's try one more. [She writes $15 \div 3 = 10 - 5$.] Is this true?

Rebecca: Yes, it's true because fifteen divided by three equals five, and ten minus five equals five, so both sides of the equal sign equal five.

Mrs. Fowle: What, then, does the equal sign mean?

Maria: It means that whatever is on one side of the equal sign must be worth the same as what's on the other side of it.

Mrs. Fowle: Exactly. The equal sign balances what's on each side. They must be equal in value, even if they don't look the same. That's why you can write fifteen equals *n* plus seven, because each side of the equation is equal in value. In your math journal, write an equation and explain what the equal sign means in that equation.

This conversation highlights a misconception that must be cleared up before equations have real meaning for students. Certainly, without this fundamental understanding of what the equal sign represents, students will struggle with algebraic concepts and higher math. By simply assessing students' understanding of this concept through informal conversation and then asking them to process what they've learned through journal writing, we can help ensure that they master this very basic concept.

Once we are comfortable that our students understand what an equation is, including what its parts represent, and that they have constructed their own knowledge and understanding about a concept, then we can begin to introduce symbols and equations associated with certain concepts. For example, in the primary grades, we talk about putting groups together and counting the total. We do this over and over with manipulatives before we introduce the symbols + and =. However, once students fully understand that when we put groups together, we are adding, then they can rely on using those symbols to create equations associated with that action.

By sixth grade, most students have been exposed to algebraic concepts, such as solving for an unknown *n*; for example, $n = 25 \times 4$, or $100 - n = 40$. These equations have no meaning to students if they have not yet mastered the concept of what the equal sign means, as mentioned previously, or what each of the other symbols ($\times$, $-$, etc.) signifies. Once students have a deep understanding of these basic symbols, they have the power to create their own equations to interpret the world around them. For example, consider this problem:

A plant grows 2.75 centimeters a day. How tall will it be on the third day? On the eighth day? Write an equation that shows how tall the plant will be on the *n*th day.

Students may choose to create a table, such as the one in Figure 4–5, showing the height of the plant each day so that they can clearly see that on day one, the plant is 2.75 centimeters, on day two, it is 5.5 centimeters, on day three, it is 8.25 centimeters, and so on. Then, they can create the equation $n \times 2.755 = $ height of plant in centimeters. A pattern has been discovered and an equation has been created to explain the pattern. That is powerful mathematical thinking!

Numbers and symbols also serve to reduce the cognitive demands on the learner. For example, when working to solve a complex problem, students can use numbers and symbols to record intermediary steps without having to remember them. They can then refer back to the notes they made when they need them.

Day	Height in Centimeters
1	2.75
2	5.5
3	8.25
4	11

Figure 4–5 *Chart showing plant's growth*

The Role of the Teacher

In the area of numbers and symbols, the teacher acts as a coach, paying careful attention to the moment when a student is ready to move from concrete representations to more abstract ones. For us to be able to do this, we must provide our students with many opportunities to show what they understand about a topic through manipulatives, paper representations, and verbal explanations. They also must be exposed to different ways of solving problems so that they can compare their strategies with others and refine theirs to an efficient, meaningful strategy upon which they can draw in the future. Equations help to form complete pictures and explain actions through symbols. For example, the equation $824 \div 22 =$ ____ means 824 divided into 22 equal groups or into groups of 22. Allowing students to use the shortcut of symbols and equations must not be the result of shortcutting them through the process of developing their own understanding of mathematical concepts and ideas. The time we spend in concept development, assessment, and determining the right moment to introduce numbers and symbols is time well invested and will help to develop competent, confident young mathematicians.

One of the most important roles of the mathematics teacher is requiring students to justify their thinking. It is not enough for students simply to give an answer. We must challenge them to defend the strategy they chose to solve a problem and to prove that they are right. Questions we might ask to accomplish this include:

■ How did you solve this problem?

■ Why did you choose that strategy?

■ Why do you think you're right?

■ How else could you have solved it?

By pushing our students to think beyond just getting the right answer, we are helping them to think more deeply about the mathematics they are learning.

Questions for Discussion

1. How can we help students make the connection between concrete and symbolic representations?

2. What is the value of alternative, or invented, algorithms?

3 How can we ensure students have a deep understanding of a concept before moving them to symbolic representations?

4. What is the value in asking students to justify their thinking?

5. What is the role of the teacher in introducing numbers and symbols to students?

5

Using Tables and Graphs to Record, Organize, and Communicate Ideas

It's Not Just About Bar Graphs Anymore!

How many times do we ask students to create a graph of their choice to represent data, only to get one bar graph after another? Have you ever looked at data displays in science or social studies and seen histograms, stem-and-leaf plots or box-and-whiskers? Not likely! Bar graphs and, in some cases, line graphs seem to be the data display most teachers use and most students feel comfortable using, regardless of whether the graph is an appropriate form for representing the data. For elementary students, bar graphs and tally charts are familiar territory. But just as with numbers, data and data displays increase in complexity as students improve their mathematical knowledge. Students need to understand that what they are graphing helps determine how they will graph the information and that some displays are not appropriate for certain data types. In this chapter, we take a look at some ways to incorporate a variety of graphing displays and then look at the analysis that needs to take place once the graphing is complete.

The standards-based classroom may at times seem limited in the type of graphing display that is promoted at a given grade level. Students in grades 6 through 8 are moving from simple bar graphs, tally charts, and line graphs to double-bar graphs, double-line graphs, line plots, stem-and-leaf plots, histograms, scatter plots, and box-and-whiskers. There are two important points to keep in mind: Once a graph has been taught, it should continue to be used and it should continue to be a choice when students are determining the most appropriate display to represent their data.

Why Graph?

Are we asking students to graph for the sake of graphing, or are we asking them to graph to answer a legitimate question? The purpose of graphing is to organize and represent data in a meaningful display to make analysis of the data easier. The purpose of collecting data is to answer a question or questions. According to NCTM, students at this grade level need to "formulate questions that can be addressed with data and collect, organize, and display relevant data to answer them" (NCTM 2002, 177). The numbers aren't a set of disconnected pieces of information created solely to practice finding mean, median, and mode. Data are information—information gathered in an attempt to see a trend, solve a problem, or support a hypothesis.

Students in grades 6 through 8 have a lot of interests that can be tapped for the purposes of learning about statistical displays. In addition, by including mathematical simulations in the classroom, a wealth of data to use statistically can be collected, but far too often, students are limited to working with meaningless sets of numbers. When this happens, little knowledge can be gained concerning the appropriate selection of the statistical display, and little knowledge is gained concerning the information the graph reveals beyond the arbitrary numbers used. Imagine the excitement that can be generated when students begin to see statistical representations about information they have gathered or about topics of interest to them. When students have a stake in the data and an interest in the question being investigated, their analysis of the data becomes much more than a series of numbers generated to find measures of central tendency. Topics for surveys with possible graphing situations include:

What is your favorite color?
What type of music do you like best?
What is your favorite sport to play?
What is your favorite sport to watch?
What is your favorite flavor of ice cream?
What is your favorite food?
What kind of pets do you have?

No matter what the topic, remember to begin with a question, and once the data are collected and displayed, use the display to answer the question. Data can be recycled, so keep collected data for those times throughout the year when students either don't have the time to collect new data or as a way to show how new displays compare to previously created graphs.

CLASSROOM-TESTED TIP

Creating and administering a survey with a large data base (such as 225 students) would take more time than most teachers want to spend on any one activity, but there are other ways to collect data. For instance, why not use a number cube, assigning each survey choice to a number? Blank cubes (see Figure 5–1) can also be used, and stickers can be affixed to the sides of the cubes. Students can then write the names of the categories on the stickers and roll the die to collect their data. Spinners can also be used for this purpose. Clear overhead spinners can be placed on top of predrawn templates with categories written in each of the spaces.

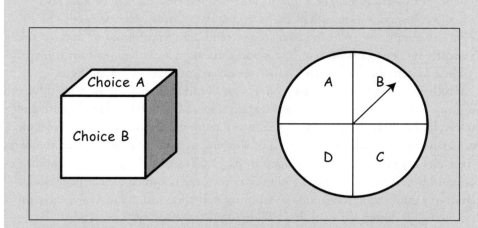

Figure 5–1 *Cubes or spinners can be used to collect data.*

Histograms and Box-and-Whiskers

Introduced at the middle grades level, histograms might best be described as bar graphs with no spaces between the bars. Many textbooks and newspapers today use histograms to display data because one of the many unique features of this display is that it really does provide a pictorial representation of all of the data. Histograms show a picture of the overall shape of the data, the symmetry of the data, outliers, and any clustering that may be present in the data. Students using a histogram to represent data will need to make a number of decisions before construction occurs. Because data in a histogram are assigned to a bin, students need to first understand how to establish intervals that are plotted along the x-axis. The height of each bar is then determined by the frequency of the data within that interval. When data sets become too large to manage with stem-and-leaf plots, a histogram is a good alternative. Although unlike stem-and-leaf plots you cannot see individual pieces of data, analyzing the shape of the histogram provides students with some real insight as to the meaning of the information displayed. Once students have an understanding of how the graph is designed, they can make use of their graphing calculator to create the display.

Like the histogram, the box-and-whiskers plot, or box plot as it is sometimes called, provides a visual summary of the data. While the histogram provides a graphic summary of the shape of the data's distribution, the box-and-whiskers plot summarizes key statistical measures. For that reason, these two displays are sometimes used together to get a complete picture of the data. Making a box-and-whiskers plot is very simple. Students only need to take the data points, organize them in order, and find the median. The median divides the data into two halves, at which point finding the median of each half provides the lower and upper quartiles. The final step is to connect with "whiskers" the lower and upper quartiles to the lower and upper extremes. Again, this type of display is much better suited to large data sets and when specific information about individual points is not needed.

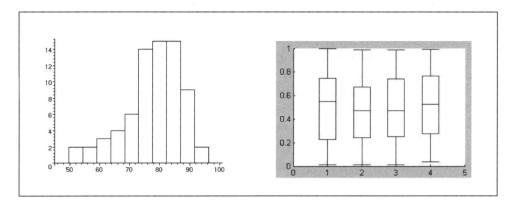

Figure 5–2 *Histogram and box-and-whiskers plot*

Line Plots or Line Graphs

For students to understand when to use appropriate data displays, they must be given multiple opportunities to see how the graphs differ in purpose. A student who uses a line graph to graph a class' preferences for food in a cafeteria obviously doesn't understand the real use of a line graph. Likewise, a student who uses a bar graph to show hourly temperature changes hasn't quite grasped the intent of a bar graph.

A line plot allows students an opportunity to count objects on a numeric scale. Generally speaking, an *X* is placed above the numeric value to represent each piece of data. Because the line plot can be compared with a bar graph, students have little trouble making the connection between the two. Line plots are actually fun for most students to create, especially when a creative teacher decides to use something other than *X*s to represent the data points. Line plots also lend themselves to other curricular topics and can be used any time you are looking to see each piece of data.

One example of how a line plot can add an element of fun to a math class can be found on the candy shelf of any grocery store. During many holiday seasons, candy makers market miniature packages with small pieces of candy. These packages can be used to practice estimation skills as well as to create graphs with real-world materials. Each student begins by estimating how many items are in the bag and then counts the items in the bag. Using a number line, students place their bag above the appropriate spot that corresponds with the number of items in their bag. Once everyone has placed their bag on the graph, the line plot takes shape. Using the bags as markers on the line plot instead of *X*s adds another element of relevance to the math being used. Keep in mind that the purpose of collecting data is to answer a question, so instead of just graphing for the sake of graphing, the teacher needs to create a legitimate question. The question could center on the weight of the bags and the number of candies inside or the price relationship to the regular-size candy bags. Whatever the question, make sure that the data collected are appropriate and provide information that will allow students the opportunity to make an informed conclusion. Students can represent the data on paper as well, substituting *X*s for the bags as they create their own graphs. If you ask students to imagine the line plot turned on its side, most will be able to see how similar it looks to a bar graph. Measures of central tendency are fairly easy to determine with a line plot.

One advantage to using a line plot is that when you are done, the data are already in order, and students will have no problem recognizing the mode and finding the median. As an extension to this activity, ask the class to apply the information gained concerning the smaller packages to estimate how many candies would be in the larger packages. Marilyn Burns has a wonderful description of a line plot activity in her book *A Collection of Math Lessons, from Grades 3 through 6* (1987). In the activity, students create line plots with small boxes of raisins (a much healthier way of collecting data). Here again, the teacher can have the students put a piece of tape on the back of their boxes and use them to graph the points on the line plot instead of using *X*s.

Continuous line graphs are different from line plots, but many times, students fail to see that difference. While a line plot counts data along a numeric scale, a continuous line graph shows pieces of data along a scale but takes it one step further and connects the pieces of data to show additional data between the points. The connecting lines often cause confusion among students if they don't realize that the lines, too, are pieces of data. An easy way to help students understand this would be to graph temperature changes, growth of a plant, or changes in the length of a shadow. By recording the data on temperature, students should see that the temperature or height gradually changes throughout the timespan being recorded and doesn't just suddenly jump to the next piece of graphed data.

Once students see the connection between the pieces of data, they should begin to see that certain types of data cannot be graphed using continuous line graphs. For example, you can't graph the number of students in your class who have computers using a continuous line plot, but students could go to a website for information on how the average number of computers owned by a family has changed over the past twenty years and graph that information. You can't graph the amount of money items cost in a grocery store on a line graph, but you can research prices of some common items and graph the price changes that have occurred over time. There are some great websites for helping students collect data for graphing change over time.

- The U.S. Census Bureau website has great data from the 2000 census (www.census.gov).

- The Central Intelligence Agency has a *World Factbook* that contains data on a number of topics, including how many telephones a country has (www.cia.gov/cia/publications/factbook/index.html).

- The U.S. Department of Agriculture site lists information on all fifty states relevant to population, farming, and exports, among other topics (www.ers.usda.gov/statefacts).

- Information on weather statistics can be found on the National Oceanic and Atmospheric Administration website from the National Climatic Data Center (www.ncdc.noaa.gov/oa/ncdc.html).

- Data on the solar system can be found at www.nineplanets.org/data.html.

Try Working Backward

Another way to help students understand continuous line graphs would be to work backward and start with the graph. Then ask students to make up the situation that might have been used to create the graph in the first place. Students in Mrs. Hamilton's sixth-grade class were given the graph in Figure 5–3 and asked to create a story about what data might have been collected to create this graph.

Patty's group wrote that they thought the graph represented a roller-coaster ride. The height of the coaster was being measured as it climbed up and then dropped down. Daryl's group concluded that it was a graph of a skateboarder, and the height of his jump was being measured as he jumped over ramps. The dip in the middle must have been when he fell from a jump. Trish's group wrote that they knew it must be measuring the loudness of the muffler on a car as it warms up in the morning. The dip might be after it cut out once before starting again.

Each group expressed ideas in broad terms, but each identified a correct situation in which a line graph might be used. This type of activity allows students to look closely at the graph and analyze the peaks and valleys for the type of information that might have been used to create the graph. This activity could also be extended by having students create their own blank graphs for others to analyze or challenging students to draw a graph that might represent a certain situation.

As students collect data for representation on any line graph, they also need to be aware of the scale that should be used and the appropriate use of each axis. It does make a difference. When students are graphing change over a period of time, the horizontal (x) axis needs to be labeled for time and the vertical (y) axis needs to be scaled for the measured data, whatever they may be. The graphs are read left to right so that the change over the period of time can be seen. Line graphs also provide wonderful opportunities to make predictions based on the shape of the line as the two pieces of data are graphed. The trends or the direction the line seems to be taking on a line graph can provide opportunities for additional conversations about predictions on what will happen in five or ten years.

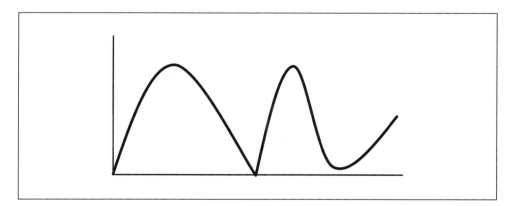

Figure 5–3 *Working backward with a line graph*

Stem-and-Leaf Plots

In addition to line plots and line graphs, stem-and-leaf plots also show all of the data points. The difference here is in the way the points are represented on the stem and leaf. Instead of a typical graph display, the stem-and-leaf represents the values of each data point using the numbers themselves. For example, to start a stem-and-leaf, a student would first need to determine the stem. It might be a single digit, or it might be larger. If the data to be graphed ranged from eleven to ninety-nine, then the stems would all be single digits starting with at least one (which represents the tens place in the number twelve). The leaves would then represent the ones place and need to be opposite the ten values. An easy data set to collect is the pulse rates of students. Most middle grades students would have no trouble working together counting pulse rates with a stopwatch. Figure 5–4 shows how collected data would look on a stem-and-leaf.

The same can be done for larger numbers; the stem would just increase in the number of digits to allow for the larger values. In later grades, students will work with back-to-back stem-and-leaf plots to allow for comparisons of two sets of data.

Because all of the data points are represented on the stem-and-leaf graph, the shape of the data becomes an important piece of the data conversation. Students may even comment that the leaves on the graph could be made to look like bars if they were shaded in and rotated. Students should be encouraged to look at the data and think about the following questions: How much of the data is in the middle? Are there any outliers that would skew the overall measures of the data? Does the data seem to be equally spaced, or are there gaps in the numbers? Having these conversations about the shape of the data instead of only looking at mean, median, and mode as descriptors of the data helps students have a better understanding of the data as a whole.

Data: 66, 72, 74, 84, 86, 87, 88, 88, 92, 94, 95, 99, 100, 102	
Stem	Leaf
5	
6	6
7	2, 4
8	4, 6, 7, 8, 8
9	2, 4, 5, 9
10	0, 2

KEY: $\boxed{7}\boxed{2}$ = 72

In this example, students did not need to start the stem with five since no number was less than sixty-three, although it is perfectly fine to do so. Notice that the data in each of the leaves are in order from least to greatest as they move away from the stem. It is easy to identify the mode, and finding the median would be just as easy because the data are already ordered.

Figure 5–4 *Stem-and-leaf plot*

Leaf	Stem	Leaf
8 3 2 0	5	
7 6 2	6	6
4 4 4 3	7	2 4
9 6 2	8	4 6 7 8 9
	9	2 4 5 9
	10	0 2

Pulse rate before exercise   Pulse rate after exercise

KEY

$\boxed{2}\boxed{8}$ = 82 $\boxed{8}\boxed{4}$ = 84

Figure 5–5 *Back-to-back stem-and-leaf of pulse rates*

Other topics that lend themselves to stem-and-leaf plots are

- ages of presidents at the time they took office or their ages at their death

- quiz or test scores

- number of books read by students during the summer

Students with an understanding of stem-and-leaf plots should easily be able to make the connection to histograms because both are frequency tables. Two sets of data can be compared with a back-to-back stem-and-leaf plot. Using the same stem, the leaves for the second set of data would move away from the stem in order as in Figure 5–5.

CLASSROOM-TESTED TIP

To create a profile of students at the beginning of the year, many teachers take an interest survey to see what sports, TV shows, music, subjects, or foods they like best. Use these surveys to tap into student interests as graphing discussions occur.

Circle Graphs

Helping students represent circle graphs (pie graphs) in grades 6 through 8 is many times done within the chapters on percentages or ratios because a circle graph shows the ratio of each segment to the whole. Although there are a number of commercially produced graphing programs available that make the job a lot easier, producing circle graphs can be a little tricky for students. There is, however, a good rationale for using circle graphs with students in these grades. Circle graphs help students visualize the relationships of the sizes of the subgroups independently or combined with each other and with the whole. Identifying the whole is much easier with a circle graph because the circle itself represents the whole. Another key aspect of the circle graph is that while it looks much different from the bar graph, the two can be used to represent the same type of data. In fact, since students are so familiar with bar graphs, using them to help students understand circle graphs makes sense.

The Role of the Teacher

In the area of graphic representations, one of the most important roles a teacher can play is in getting students to see the differences in purpose of certain graphs and how crucial it is to choose the correct representation for the information at hand. Yes, we all know the importance of placing a title on a graph and labeling the x- and y-axes because that gives important information to the reader, but is it more important than using the appropriate type of graph? Teachers also need to ensure that their students have opportunities to look at data collection and representation of those data as part of a question to be answered. A list of arbitrary numbers to graph does not help students see the importance of graphic display and data analysis. So-called naked math serves no purpose in helping students internalize these concepts. Graphing needs to be in context with choices. In the area of data analysis, students can take a lot more meaning away from mean, median, and mode when context is used, but those are not the only analyses of the data and graph that need to take place. In addition to the measures of central tendency, teachers should help students analyze the graph in other ways. By asking questions about the shape of the graphed data or how far apart the data points are, teachers can help students begin to see information about the population being graphed even before they perform computations on the data.

The Role of Technology

Using a computer or graphing calculator sounds like an easy solution to time-intensive graphic displays. The problem with the use of technology is that it doesn't tell you whether or not the graph selected is appropriate. Graphing software will take the data and configure them into the display chosen by the user. For this reason, caution needs to be exercised when allowing students free choice in the graph to use. Continue to remind students that information may not be useful if the incorrect graph is chosen.

Questions for Discussion

1. How can allowing student choice in graphic display provide information on students' understanding of the purpose of each graph?

2. Why is it important to look at data collection as a means for answering a question?

Figure 5-6 *Computers provide a variety of software applications for graphing.*

3. How can teachers help students in connecting the uses and purposes of the various graphic displays?

4. What are some of the steps that can be used as students are led through the concrete to the symbolic stages of graphing?

5. What are some of the reasons students need context in graphing?

6

Assessing Students' Representations

Assessment is the process of gathering evidence about a student's knowledge of, ability to use, and disposition toward, mathematics and of making inferences from that evidence for a variety of purposes.

—National Council of Teachers of Mathematics,
Assessment Standards for School Mathematics

The ability to represent math ideas in multiple ways is extremely useful as students grow in their mathematical knowledge. By being able to draw on words, pictures, numbers, tables, and so on, students are empowered to understand and represent the world around them and their internal thought processes. However, these models that serve as a student's toolbox must be constructed because they are not taught or given by the teacher. Rather, they emerge from a student's actions in a given situation. When faced with the issue of assessing our students' representations, we must ask ourselves two questions: Why are we assessing the representations our students make? How are we going to use the information gained from the assessment tool? In this chapter, we discuss the value in assessing those representations, and we look at different ways we can assess our students.

Why Assess?

Teachers assess every day, either formally or informally, and for different reasons. Our most common assessment is that which helps us to make decisions about our instruction. We make daily adjustments to our plans based on our students' needs. Do some students need additional time to explore a topic? Are some students ready to move forward with the application of the concept? Have a group of students demonstrated mastery, and do they need to be challenged? Are the majority of students confused about a topic, and do they need a new approach? Assessment is essential in helping us make these decisions.

Another reason we assess is to give parents and students feedback. Most students want to know where they excel and where they need to improve. Parents are especially interested in how their child is performing in relationship to other students as well as the grade-level content. Assessment (especially performance assessment) can help us give them this information. By seeing how they do when faced with a task with specific objectives, students can get a clear idea of their performance at any given moment. Finally, we may use assessment to help us assign a grade to a student's performance. Evaluating student learning is a complex task that is supported by quality assessment, which can be used to justify a teacher's decision to assign a certain grade to a student.

Assessing Representation

In grades 6 through 8, the main goal of the representation process standard is simply to be able to represent the mathematics and represent student understanding of the mathematics. Many students will become competent at representing and will look for more accurate and efficient ways to do so, but some students will still struggle with what it means to make a representation of their thinking. We all strive to help our students become proficient in mathematics, and all teachers want to judge fairly the work put forth by students. How, then, do we assess students' ability to represent their thinking? In this book, we have been looking at how students can represent their thinking in a number of ways. Words, pictures, diagrams, symbols, and numbers are all elements of what we have been calling multiple representations. But when we assess students' representations, are we looking for the correctness of their answers? Are we looking for an appropriate algorithm that can be used to solve a problem? Are we looking to see what steps the student went through to reach a solution? Are we assessing only what they could put down on paper? Are we assessing the conceptual understandings or the procedural ones? And finally, what tools do we use in assessing student representations?

Math classrooms today bear little resemblance to classrooms ten to fifteen years ago. Gone are the days when students were asked to solve problems without justifying their thinking. Students today are required to demonstrate their thinking and reasoning through explanations and justifications of their work. We are being challenged to find and use assessments that are rich and have the range of uses that will allow students an opportunity to demonstrate their levels of understanding. If a task is not rich, if it is not cognitively demanding, then students will not be able to adequately demonstrate their knowledge. What information will we gain from a task that has only a right or wrong answer? Today, more than ever, information about students' levels of understanding and mastery is all too important as we look for ways to adjust our instruction to meet the needs of not only our curriculum but more important our students.

We have a number of valuable options available when assessing students' representations. We might

■ observe students and engage them in conversations about their work

■ interview and conference with students

■ use a performance-based task

■ collect samples of their work (e.g., portfolios)

The questions are: What should we assess? and When should we assess? Choosing the correct assessment is determined by our purpose in assessing, as described earlier. In this chapter, we look at different forms of assessment and determine how we might use them when looking at our students' representations.

Observations

During a math lesson, it is not uncommon for us to walk around and see what our students are doing. Are they on task? Do they appear excited, frustrated, or confused about the activity? Are they working purposefully or merely attempting to appear busy?

Ongoing observations give teachers opportunities to see students in a variety of situations during the math class, and while most of those observations are informal in nature, they should be a part of the regular classroom routine. The important thing to remember is the documentation that needs to take place during that observation time or shortly thereafter. Without some form of documentation, those mental notes we make as we walk around the room become lost and may fail to provide any lasting information.

One way to make the classroom observation meaningful is to structure a task in which all students are engaged in the same topic at the same time. When planning that task, the teacher needs to create a few focused questions to ask during this time and determine how the information will be documented.

Sixth-grade teacher Mrs. Turner engages in what she likes to call "clipboard cruising." As students are working on an activity, whether cooperatively or independently, she walks around the room with her clipboard, a set of sticky notes, and focus questions. Stopping by Karen's desk, she asks, "How does your representation of the first part of this problem match the question?" If Karen is able to connect her notations to the problem in a meaningful way or if she has created a picture that shows an appropriate level of mastery, Mrs. Turner notes that on Karen's card or sticky note.

She may ask one question or a series of questions, but she is always trying to get the students to explain their thinking as they work through the task. Other questions she might ask include: "How is your representation of this solution similar to (or different from) one you did yesterday?" "Can you explain the picture you drew for this part of the problem?" and "Why did you choose to organize your work in this way?"

As students respond to her questions, she quickly jots down some of their responses on their sticky note. If a student can justify his representation of the problem, if he can provide evidence that he has used his representations to make the problem more meaningful or to find a solution, she makes quick notes of his efforts. She can also clearly see when a student is unable to adequately justify a response or when the representations seem to be taking the student in another direction, indicating that the teacher needs to find a way to redirect the student's thinking. Once class is over, she either adds to her notes if time allows or files them in student or class folders for later.

Mrs. Turner is looking for a number of things as she cruises the room: Is student work organized, have the students been able to communicate their thinking, and have they chosen to use one of the problem-solving strategies appropriate for this problem? The observation is purposeful, it is organized, and because Mrs. Turner records the information, it provides lasting evidence of student work. She won't get to all students every day, but it has become a part of her classroom routine, and students know what to expect and aren't surprised or caught off guard when she stops by their desk.

Interviews and Conferences

In addition to observing students as they work, having a structured time to meet and confer with students one on one concerning their progress provides valuable information. Planned conferences allow for a much more structured venue for engaging students in math conversations. Although finding the time to have these conversations or interviews with students may be difficult, teachers are wonderfully creative in utilizing stolen moments of time, especially when their efforts yield lasting results.

In Mr. Cody's eighth-grade class, he has regularly scheduled interview times with students during lunch periods, scheduled times at the end of class periods, and before or after school when he can focus on a particular student. He starts early in the year talking with his students about the interview process and has an introductory meeting lasting only five to ten minutes when he asks them about their attitudes concerning math. He also likes to see what areas they feel are strengths and/or weaknesses. Keeping the interview short and nonthreatening is essential to having students feel comfortable and willing to talk about their perceived abilities. He tries to make sure he asks each student the same or at least similar questions so that he has like information on each student.

As the year progresses, he continues with both formal and informal interviews with his students. Sometimes, his inquiries are about a particular task, and he may ask them questions such as, "Why did you choose this representation?" and "Was there another way to solve that problem?" He wants his students to look at alternative methods of solving problems and representing the solutions, so he encourages them to always look back and rethink the problems instead of being satisfied with one method.

In an interview with Jenna on her work with the Raking Leaves activity, Mr. Cody was particularly interested in how Jenna handled the first portion of the task. He wasn't able to see Jenna's thinking, so he asked her how she determined the total time written as a fraction that Charlie spent working in the yard. (See Figure 6–1.)

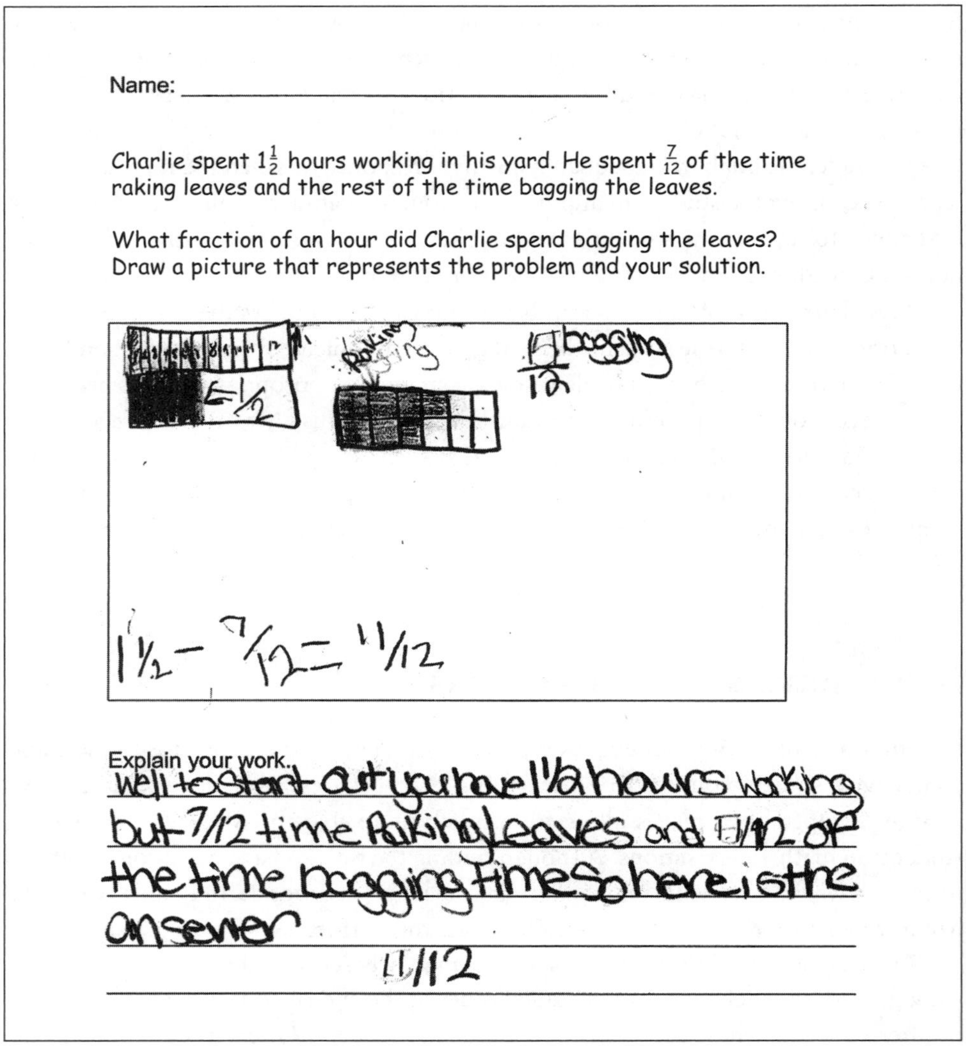
Name: ____________________.
Charlie spent $1\frac{1}{2}$ hours working in his yard. He spent $\frac{7}{12}$ of the time raking leaves and the rest of the time bagging the leaves.
What fraction of an hour did Charlie spend bagging the leaves? Draw a picture that represents the problem and your solution.
=1/2
Raking
bagging
5/12 bagging
1 1/2 − 7/12 = 11/12
Explain your work.
Well to start out you have 1 1/2 hours working but 7/12 time Raking leaves and 5/12 of the time bagging times so here is the ansewer
11/12

Figure 6–1 *Jenna's work on Raking Leaves*

Jenna explained that since the problem told her that Charlie spent $\frac{7}{12}$ of his time raking leaves, she wanted to create an equivalent fraction for the $1\frac{1}{2}$ hours that would allow her to subtract without regrouping or having to find a common denominator. She knew that $\frac{12}{12}$ was equal to one whole and $\frac{1}{2}$ of an hour was the same as $\frac{6}{12}$, so together she had $\frac{18}{12}$. Once she had the improper fraction, she just subtracted out the $\frac{7}{12}$, giving her and answer of $\frac{11}{12}$. It was clear that Jenna had internalized the process, and her drawing confirmed her discussion with Mr. Cody, but without taking time to question the procedure, Mr. Cody wouldn't have had some additional insight into her thinking.

Interviews can be wonderfully enlightening, and taking the time out of a busy schedule to meet one on one with students to discuss their work has huge payoffs in the end.

Performance-Based Tasks

Developing a good performance-based task is sometimes easier said than done. What we think will make a rich question for students to explore sometimes fails to address the mathematics as much as we would like. A performance-based task implies that we want the students to do something and we have identified a product that will serve as proof they have accomplished that task. However, doing an activity for the sake of doing an activity without attention to the mathematics involved is a waste of everyone's time.

The first decision a teacher has to make in determining what type of activity to do is what the math is. The second decision must be about the best way to address the concept and whether or not students will be able to demonstrate their knowledge. Performance tasks are not easy to assess unless the teacher has thought through all of the steps prior to assigning them, and even then, adjustments may be needed once students start working. We are sometimes surprised when we see what students actually read into the problems. An effective task must be relevant to the math, be rich in context, and provide opportunities for students to display their level of thinking.

Scoring tasks can sometimes be done with a generic rubric or a task-specific checklist. Whatever the criteria, students should be made aware of the criteria prior to starting the task. If the intent of the task is to get at multiple representations of the problem, then that must be a part of the scoring criteria. Some teachers prefer to score tasks in a holistic fashion. This means that when they create their rubric or scoring checklist, the elements within the tool apply to the whole product rather than a single element. For example, in a holistic rubric, a teacher might identify three to four elements that can be scored. These elements would all be grouped together, and they would apply to the entire performance, not to individual pieces of that performance. Elements might include items such as completing the task, demonstrating understanding, and showing appropriate representations. The degree to which the student accomplished these elements would then determine his or her score.

In an analytic rubric, individual elements and the degree to which each is achieved are scored separately. For example, did the student demonstrate understanding of the problem and to what degree? Did the student make a plan to solve the problem and to what degree? Whether holistic or analytic, the rubric needs to have as one of its elements descriptions of how the representations will be scored. An element on a rubric associated with representations might read: "Communicates thinking clearly, using appropriate words, computation, diagrams, charts, or other representations." If students know ahead of time that the representation element is equally as important as the answer, they can attend to that portion of their response.

Rubrics used in scoring tasks should be easy to apply, and the score should not be difficult to determine. The more opportunities students have to be assessed using a rubric, the more comfortable they'll become with the process. If a task-specific scoring tool is needed, you can create a checklist that resembles the rubric but has specific information about that one assignment.

Pinch Card Scoring

Use index cards and write the numbers 0, 1, 2, and 3 down the side. As you walk around the room and observe students at work either independently or in small groups, you can pinch a card next to the score you would give their work at that point and hand the card to the student or group. This way, no other students become aware of the score, and the student can get quick feedback on his or her efforts and adjust as necessary. You can also make cards for students so that they can self-score their efforts.

Portfolios: Collections of Student Work

Portfolios allow students an opportunity to showcase their work. They also provide teachers and parents with a picture album that summarizes a student's progress and efforts. Assessments should not be snapshots in time; rather, they should capture a student at various places along his or her learning continuum. By carefully structuring the collection of student work, a teacher can gather evidence of growth and information on how a student's mathematical thinking has developed. Portfolios of student work need to be structured from the start. It isn't enough to ask students to put evidence of their work in a folder. Instead, we need to be clear about what type of work we expect students to submit. For that reason, it is important to list for students some of the criteria they need to consider as they select work samples. In the area of representations, we want the students to select work that shows both their thinking and their ability to use multiple representations. They need to include samples of work that show that they

- used pictures to help them reach a solution

- used graphic representations of the data (more than one sample)

- used words to explain how they developed their solution

- used words to justify why their solution was correct

- used a graphic organizer to illustrate a procedure

- used more than one representation to reach their solution

- worked with a group to solve a problem

If the criteria for assessing the portfolio collection are made clear to the students beforehand and they have a checklist of desired elements, they can begin assembling their work at the start of the school year. If they find better examples of a certain type of work, they can replace previous selections.

In Mrs. Waller's sixth-grade class, her students regularly update and add to their portfolio collections. She hands each student a criteria checklist at the beginning of the year and goes over how they are to select work samples for their portfolios. She also lists some required pieces, such as formative assessment samples and journal entries on certain topics. The students are ultimately responsible for the rest of the collection. At the end of the year, she has her students go through their portfolios one more time to review all of the pieces they have chosen. At that time, she asks each student to select one piece of work that he or she is proudest of creating, and she invites parents in for an afternoon of sharing portfolio samples.

Parents first walk around the room, looking at the various pieces of student work, and then she has each student present the one sample that they chose from all of their work pieces. The students explain why this is a good work sample and what they have learned from the assignment. Then they show how the sample meets the criteria. This activity creates wonderful communication among students, the teacher, and parents, and at the same time, it provides additional motivation for the students in making careful selections along the way because they know their parents will be in to look through all of the samples. At the end of the gallery walk, Mrs. Waller encourages parents to take their child's collection of work samples and share it with the next year's teacher at an appropriate time.

Assessment Equity

With the growing trend toward full inclusion, teachers today have more challenges than ever in making sure students are assessed fairly and equitably. All students must be assessed. The question is: How do you assess students with special needs and report their performance with clarity? In assessing representations, the answer may be a little easier than in other areas because alternative representations do in fact have a tendency to meet the needs of our special learners.

- Provide a frame or context for the problem: Many of our lesson plans and assessment documents can be adapted so students can answer in an alternative form. For example, instead of asking a student to answer a question such as, "Which is greater, four-fifths or five-fourths?" you can ask the student to place the two fractions on a number line. By asking the question in this manner and providing the number, you present the student with a framework for the question, which may allow him or her to more easily determine which fraction is larger when considering its placement on a number line. You might also ask the student to represent the two fractions in a drawing, which would give you even more information about the student's understanding of the relative size of the two fractions.

- Use manipulatives: Continue the availability of manipulatives during assessments. By making classroom tools available during assessment time, you help all students feel comfortable accessing them as they work through problems. The students can work the solutions out using the manipulatives and then make the appropriate representations on the paper.

■ Conduct group assessments: Consider allowing students to take an assessment as a group. In this type of assessment, students will feel free to discuss the mathematics and also show each other how they would represent their ideas either pictorially or numerically.

■ Make use of technology: There are a number of opportunities today to have students demonstrate their knowledge using technology. Teachers can make use of virtual manipulatives to help students solve problems and then have them translate the pictures to their own work.

Feedback

The purpose of assessment is to provide information, and that information needs to be used to inform instruction. What do we do with the evidence we collect on our students' performance? We can begin by asking questions about some of the student work we collect. Have the students communicated their solutions with appropriate words, numbers, and/or pictures? What mathematical thinking is evidenced in their work? What are some of the differences in the ways students found results? We also need to be mindful of the task we have given them and ask ourselves if it provided us with the information we thought it would or if we need to revise the task to make it richer. Do we have sufficient information on how the students have performed compared with the standards, and if not, what do we need to do to help them improve? And finally, what information can we provide parents about their children?

Assessment is no longer about a grade, it is no longer about a moment in time, and it is no longer about only an answer without an explanation of process or justification for procedure. Assessment needs to be ongoing, it needs to be informative, and it needs to be accessible to all students. Having students skilled in solving problems using a variety of representation strategies is a goal that we all can set for ourselves and for our students. If we are to help students grow in the math competencies, we need to provide them with as many strategies as possible along the way. We need to continue to look for and create those assessment items that allow our students multiple pathways to achieving success.

Questions for Discussion

1. What are some of the ways students can be assessed?

2. How can student interviews provide insight into our students' thinking?

3. What advantages can be found in using rubrics for scoring tools?

4. What feedback can we supply students about their assessment data?

5. How can the use of representations help in our assessment of special needs students?

CHAPTER 7

Representations Across the Content Standards

Students in the elementary and middle grades use a variety of forms of representation to record and communicate their thinking: symbols, drawings and pictures, tables and charts, physical materials, graphs, models, and oral and written language.

—Suzanne Chapin, Catherine O'Connor, and Nancy Anderson,
Classroom Discussions: Using Math Talk to Help Students Learn

We have been focusing on helping our students develop the ability to represent their thinking and the mathematical concepts they are learning about. Being able to represent both externally and internally will enable students to approach novel situations with many strategies from which to choose. Symbols, drawings and pictures, tables and charts, graphs, manipulatives, models, and oral and written language are just some of these representations. Representation, however, is only one of five different process standards set forth by the National Council of Teachers of Mathematics (NCTM 2000). The other four include problem solving, reasoning and proof, communication, and connections. Representation is interconnected to each of these other processes. When problem solving, students might use representations in the form of pictures to help them understand the problem, and then they might represent their solution in the form of an equation. They use reasoning skills to infer and decipher information, and they might use representations to justify their answer to a problem. To communicate their thought processes, students might create a representation in the form of a diagram or an equation. Students connect math concepts to other math concepts and to the world around them, and representations such as a graph or manipulatives can help to show these connections.

Just as the process standards are interconnected, we must connect content to those process standards in a meaningful way. NCTM (2000) has outlined content standards in five areas: number and operations, algebra, geometry, measurement, and data analysis and probability. In this chapter, we look at how the representations can be developed and used across the content standards. In each section, we give an overview of a lesson or problem task related to the content standard, highlight the use of representation in the lesson or activity, and discuss the mathematics involved.

Number and Operations

Students who understand the structure of numbers and the relationships among numbers can work with them flexibly. (NCTM 2000, 149)

Students in grades 6 through 8 continue to develop number sense while working more with the concepts of multiplication, division, and rational numbers and their operations. As they grow in their understanding of these operations and become more fluent in using multiplication and division to solve a variety of problems, they begin to make generalizations that they can begin to apply when working with various operations involving decimals and fractions. The following activity was conducted in Mrs. Thompson's seventh-grade math class and required students to apply common problem-solving strategies as they looked for ways to represent a tricky problem with fractions.

The Problem Task

The Cookie Caper

One night, the king went down into the royal kitchen where he found a basket full of cookies. He was hungry, so he ate $\frac{1}{6}$ of the cookies.

Later that night, the queen went down to the royal kitchen where she found the basket of cookies, and she ate $\frac{1}{5}$ of what was left.

Still later, the prince awoke, went down to the kitchen, and ate $\frac{1}{4}$ of the cookies that were left.

Even later, his sister, the princess, went down to the kitchen. She found the basket of cookies and ate $\frac{1}{3}$ of the cookies she found.

Finally, the royal jester came by and found the cookies. He ate $\frac{1}{2}$ of the cookies he found.

The next morning, the cook came down. She found only three cookies left in the basket.

How many cookies were there originally?

Before starting work on the problem, Mrs. Thompson led the class in a discussion on possible strategies they could use in solving this problem. She was interested in seeing how many different strategies the students could apply because the problem could be solved any number of ways. The first question many of them wanted answered was about using a calculator. Tom thought it wouldn't take long to finish the problem if they could just add the numbers. Mrs. Thompson told them they could use a calculator, and they were welcome to try any strategy they wanted.

Maria thought that they could use trial and error to solve the problem since the numbers were small. She said that if they made a table of their guesses, they would be able to see if their next guess needed to be a higher or lower number. Tia offered that she wanted to solve it by working backward. She likened it to a game show where you have the answer and need to come up with the question. She said that since the problem shows how many cookies were left the next morning, the problem should be solved by starting with the three and working backward. Tom's group thought the problem could be solved by writing a series of equations that could be solved one after the other. However, they commented that it might be a lot like Tia's strategy since you would still have to start at the end of the problem. The last group to respond wanted to try drawing a diagram of the problem and seeing if they could get an answer with pictures instead of equations.

Since each group now had a strategy, Mrs. Thompson decided to let them all approach the problem in the way they had described. She encouraged them all to discuss the meaning of the problem in their cooperative groups and plan their strategy for how they were going to tackle the problem. The students had a number of manipulatives and tools at their disposal such as two-color counters, color tiles, dry-erase boards, and a sheet of easel paper with chart markers, and yes, a calculator. Each group was allowed to choose the manipulatives they thought would help them the most.

Maria's Group: Guess and Check

Since Maria's group decided to go with trial and error, they needed to plan a table that would allow them to keep track of their guesses. They drew a table with six columns, one for each person in the problem, and labeled each heading according to what they ate (Figure 7–1). The first guess they reasoned must be a multiple of six since the first thing they had to do was to multiply it by $\frac{1}{6}$, so their first guess was thirty-six. They chose this number because they thought it would be reasonable—not too big and not too small. If the king ate $\frac{1}{6}$ of the thirty-six cookies, he would have eaten six of them leaving thirty for the queen. If the queen ate $\frac{1}{5}$ of thirty cookies, she too would have eaten six cookies leaving twenty-four for the prince. The prince had twenty-four cookies when he came down, and he ate $\frac{1}{4}$ of them, and that was six more. At this point, the group was glad the fractions were coming out even, but they were a little afraid that they were doing something wrong because all of the answers were turning out to be six. In any event, they kept going. Once again, they ended up with an answer of six when they took $\frac{1}{3}$ of eighteen for the princess. This meant that the jester would have twelve cookies in the bowl when he came downstairs. If the jester ate half of the cookies, he too would eat six cookies, and the cook would have found six the next morning instead of three.

By the time they reached the end of the first guess, they had taken about ten minutes of their time. The discussion between each problem centered on the sameness of the answer for each problem. They also wanted to know if this wasn't the answer, why did all of the problems divide out evenly? In the end, they needed to decide on their next guess. Marcus decided that since the answer they got was twice as much as it needed to be, maybe they should cut their guess in half. With no other suggestions, they tried eighteen as their second guess. The table shows their results. After the problem was complete, everyone in the group decided that this method worked well for this problem, and since the second trial went much faster than the first, they finished on time.

Tia's Group: Working Backward with a Manipulative and Diagram

Tia's group chose to work the problem backward because they had a final answer. The group opted to use the two-color counters and draw a picture to help them with the problem. They started with three counters to represent the three cookies found by the cook. Looking at the problem, they decided that since three was half of six and the jester had left three after he ate half, then there must have been six cookies in the bowl when the jester came downstairs.

With a solid start, the group continued to talk through the problem and draw the counters that they had on their desk. The next statement from the problem said that the princess ate $\frac{1}{3}$ of the cookies. Brian offered that since there were six cookies left after the princess ate $\frac{1}{3}$, she must have started with nine cookies and also eaten three cookies. Charlie wasn't convinced. He asked, "How can $\frac{1}{2}$ and $\frac{1}{3}$ be the same number of cookies? Doesn't $\frac{1}{2}$ have to be more?" Tia explained that this was possible because the number of cookies changed, and $\frac{1}{2}$ of six was the same number as $\frac{1}{3}$ of nine.

The next part of the problem said that $\frac{1}{4}$ of the cookies had been eaten by the prince, which resulted in the nine cookies being left. Charlie spoke up and said, "We know that if $\frac{1}{4}$ of the cookies were eaten, then $\frac{3}{4}$ were left, and $\frac{3}{4}$ of something is equal to the nine." While the group understood the concept of $\frac{3}{4}$ remaining, they weren't quite sure how to set up the problem.

Now that they had worked all the way back to the beginning, they decided to read through the problem and see if their solution made sense. So, with Tia pointing out the steps, Charlie read the problem again.

"The king ate $\frac{1}{6}$ of the cookies and $\frac{1}{6}$ of eighteen is three, so if there were eighteen cookies to start, eighteen minus three left fifteen cookies.

"The queen ate $\frac{1}{5}$ of the remaining cookies, and $\frac{1}{5}$ of fifteen is three, and fifteen minus three equals twelve remaining cookies.

King ate $\frac{1}{6}$ of	Queen ate $\frac{1}{5}$ of	Prince ate $\frac{1}{4}$ of	Princess ate $\frac{1}{3}$ of	Jester ate $\frac{1}{2}$ of	Cook found 3 cookies
$\frac{1}{6}$ of 36 = 6	$\frac{1}{5}$ of 30 = 6	$\frac{1}{4}$ of 24 = 6	$\frac{1}{3}$ of 18 = 6	$\frac{1}{2}$ of 12 = 6	6 ≠ 3 ☒
$\frac{1}{6}$ of 18 = 3	$\frac{1}{5}$ of 15 = 3	$\frac{1}{4}$ of 12 = 3	$\frac{1}{3}$ of 9 = 3	$\frac{1}{2}$ of 6 = 3	3 = 3 ☑

Figure 7–1 *Maria's group: Guess and check method*

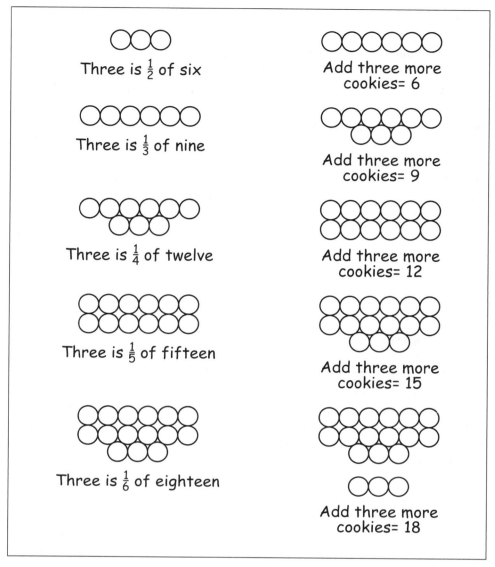

Figure 7–2 *Tia's group's completed representation of The Cookie Caper problem*

"The prince ate $\frac{1}{4}$ of the twelve cookies, and that is three, so twelve minus three equals nine cookies left.

"The princess ate $\frac{1}{3}$ of the nine remaining cookies, and that is also equal to three, so now there are six cookies, and when the jester comes down to eat $\frac{1}{2}$ of the cookies, he too only eats three."

Everyone applauded their efforts, but many were quick to say that they couldn't believe that all of those different fractions could equal the same amount.

Tom's Group: Equations

Tom's group decided that they had all the information they needed with the exception of how many cookies were in the bowl. Their variable would be m = number of cookies. The first equation on their paper was: The king ate $\frac{1}{6}m$. From this, they decided that when the king finished eating, there would be $m - \frac{1}{6}m$ left. Tom felt that they could simplify the expression by combining like terms. He said, "With the variable m by itself, it really stands for $1m$, so all we need to do is rename it $\frac{6}{6}m$." Charlotte wanted to know why they should rename it $\frac{6}{6}$ and not some other fraction. Tom explained that since the other fraction was in sixths, they needed to rename the whole using the same denominator. Simplified, the fraction would be $\frac{5}{6}m$. If the king left $\frac{5}{6}m$ for the queen, and she ate $\frac{1}{5}$ of those cookies, then when she was finished, she would have eaten $\frac{5}{6}m - \frac{1}{5}(\frac{5}{6}m)$, which would equal $\frac{4}{6}m$. Charlotte felt that at this point they might have a pattern. She said, "Each time we are repeating the same steps; we have to take a fraction of the previous answer and then subtract it from that answer. It looks like each time we do this, we get $\frac{1}{6}$ less than we started with before." After testing their rule on the prince, the princess, and the jester by subtracting $\frac{1}{6}$ from $\frac{4}{6}$ for each of them, they ended up with $\frac{1}{6}m = 3$, which meant that m would have to equal eighteen. Tom went back to the start of the problem, and the group double-checked each solution with their answer.

About the Math

Problem-solving experiences with fractions allow students opportunities to clarify concepts and skills that are all too often forgotten when students fail to internalize the processes. Even though this problem was challenging for the students, the numbers were manageable, and as the students discovered, once the pattern was spotted, the whole problem became that much easier. Charlie's insight into looking at the problem in terms of what was left when he indicated he knew $\frac{3}{4}$ remained once $\frac{1}{4}$ had been eaten, while accurate, didn't really help his group because they were unsure of how to set up the problem. As it turns out, they were able to solve the problem without the equation, while Tom's group relied solely on the equation method. At this level, it is sometimes difficult to separate the number computation from the algebra strand. Because some groups will have the ability to complete problems such as this using algebra, allowing them to do so is one way to differentiate your instruction. The problem is not different, but the process is certainly varied for each group that did this problem.

In this problem, students started out wanting to use a common tool that everyone thought would help with all math problems: the calculator. In this case, it might have helped if the students understood what numbers to input. But in this problem, they couldn't see the pattern in the solution until they started to draw it out while using the manipulatives. Students who learn early on that alternative methods of working through problems can sometimes be easier to use than a calculator will be able to apply those skills to more complex problems, provided they have opportunities to continue to practice those strategies.

> The fact that representations are such effective tools may obscure how difficult it was to develop them and more important, how much work it takes to understand them. (NCTM 2000)

Purchase packages of inexpensive plastic cups in red, yellow, and green. When students are engaged in small-group work, give them a stack of three plastic cups, one of each color. As the students are working, they should have their green cup at the top of their stack. If they begin to experience problems along the way, they need to put the yellow cup on top. The yellow cup tells you that the students are having a little trouble, but they are still working. With the yellow cup on top, students know to try to figure out how to continue without the teacher's help. The last resort is the red cup. When the red cup goes on top, it is a signal to the teacher that the group can't continue without assistance, and they need help *now*. If cups aren't available, use laminated signs in red, yellow, and green that students can put on the corner of their desk. The cups reassure the students that they can ask for help but that they need to try to work things out first. The teacher is always the last resort.

Algebra

More and more teachers are being asked to foster algebraic thinking at all grade levels. Today, the big ideas of algebra, including equivalence, properties, and variables, show up in many elementary classrooms. When students think of algebra, they think of variables, and the very abstract nature of the standard makes teaching all that much harder and intimidating. For students to understand the generalized nature of algebra, they need to see the connections to arithmetic at each grade level. For this reason, problems that provide students with opportunities to make those connections need to begin early.

The following activity, conducted in a sixth-grade class, involves figuring out three unknown quantities based on information given in the problem.

The Problem Task

The following problem was posed in a sixth-grade classroom to observe students' number sense, use of algebraic principles, and use of representation to solve the problem. With this problem task, students were immediately engaged in exploring math content through the process of problem solving.

> The sum of the ages of David, Tom, and Jim is thirty-four. David is three years older than Jim, and Tom is five years younger than Jim. Find the ages of David, Tom, and Jim.

To promote discussion about their thinking, the teacher, Mrs. Powell, asked students to work with a partner to complete the activity. After Mrs. Powell posed the problem, she asked students for their thoughts on how they would solve it. Before turning them loose to sink or swim, she wanted to make sure everyone had an idea of how they could approach the problem. Jessica offered that since they had three unknowns, maybe they should start by labeling them x, y, and z. Instead of commenting, Mrs. Powell asked the class what they thought. Most of the students seemed to agree with Jessica's idea. Mrs. Powell wasn't quite sure at this point whether this was because they really thought she was correct or because they just didn't know. Another student commented that if you gave each one of them a different variable, then you wouldn't be able to solve the problem.

Mrs. Powell wanted them to solve the problem independently, so giving additional hints at this time wasn't in her plan. Instead, she told the students to look at the problem differently. She said, "If you can use only one variable for the problem, what is it you need to know to get information about the other two people in the problem?" Students had access to counters, paper and pencils, dry-erase boards, and markers. Because the numbers in the problem were so small, she didn't provide a calculator. The computation would in no way interfere with their solving the problem. While the students worked, she circulated, listening to the students' conversations, questioning to promote thinking, and clarifying the task when necessary.

Initially, most of the students did not know where to begin with this task. Several attempted to add the different numbers in the problem even though they really didn't know why. Sam's group took their thirty-four counters and put them in three piles on the dry-erase board, and Sam said, "Since the numbers are small, maybe we can just guess at the answer." He and his partner drew circles around the three piles of counters, labeled them D, T, and J, and started counting to see if the numbers would match the problem. Their first guess was twenty, ten, and four. When they tried putting the numbers back in the problem, they quickly realized that although the numbers added up to thirty-four, they didn't match the problem in any way. Michael's group was watching Sam's attempts at guessing. He told Sam that his numbers were too far apart, "I don't know the answer, but if you look at the problem, all of the ages are fairly close to one another." He continued with, "It says in the problem that David is only three years older than Jim, and Tom is five years younger." Martha, Sam's partner, said, "That makes Tom the youngest."

Both groups had bits and pieces of information, but they were still struggling with what it all meant. This is the case many times when students try to put words into expressions and equations. Sam finally decided that since they had information about how far from Jim's age everyone else was, they would label Jim as the variable j. From here, they determined that if Jim was j, then David must be $j + 3$ because he is three years older. Michael determined that Tom must be $j - 5$ because he was five years younger.

The two groups now had the labels for the three people, and they knew that the sum of all of their ages was thirty-four, so they wrote: $j + j + 3 + j - 5 = 34$. From here, they combined their like terms to get $3j - 2 = 34$, and they added 2 to both sides and simplified the problem even further to $3j = 36$. All that remained was to divide 36 by 3 to get 12 as their answer for j. Sam said, "That makes Jim twelve years old, David fifteen years old, and Tom must be seven years old." They checked their work to make sure their answer made sense and waited to report to the rest of the class.

When it came time to share their answers, one of the other groups started by saying they made David the variable and came up with these three labels: David = d, Jim = $d - 3$, and Tom = $d - 8$. When they solved the problem, their answer was that David was fifteen years old. (See their solution in Figure 7–3.) At first, the class was confused. There were just as many groups that had done the problem both ways. In fact, a couple of groups found a third way to work through the problem, and that was to make Tom the variable.

The discussion that took place in the small groups and the whole group was lively, and many students were full of questions. This is the type of problem that seems a lot harder than it actually is. The hardest part was in translating the words into a representation that made sense to the students so they could solve the equation.

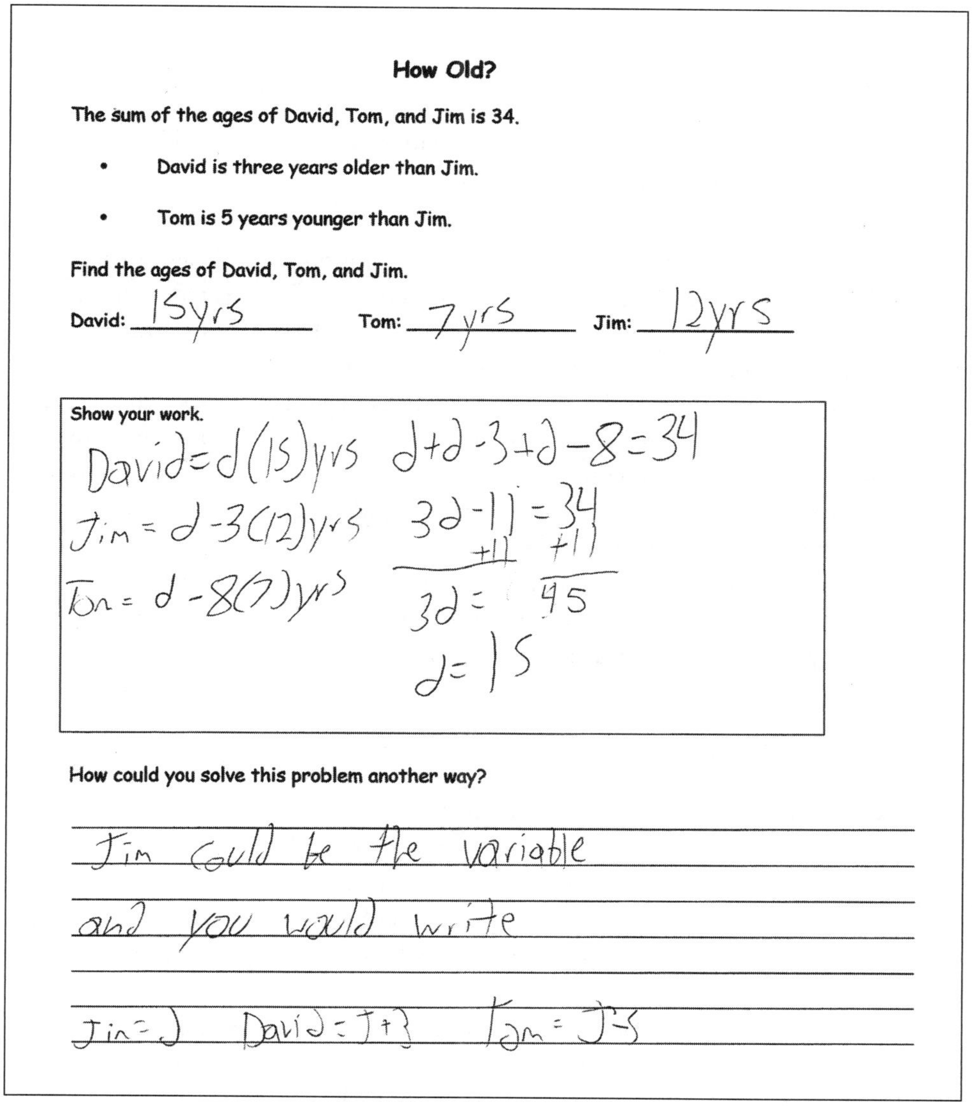

How Old?

The sum of the ages of David, Tom, and Jim is 34.

- David is three years older than Jim.

- Tom is 5 years younger than Jim.

Find the ages of David, Tom, and Jim.

David: __15 yrs__   Tom: __7 yrs__   Jim: __12 yrs__

Show your work.

David = d (15) yrs $d + d - 3 + d - 8 = 34$

Jim = d - 3 (12) yrs $3d - 11 = 34$
                         $\underset{+11}{} \quad \underset{+11}{}$

Tom = d - 8 (7) yrs $3d = 45$

                       $d = 15$

How could you solve this problem another way?

Jim could be the variable
and you would write

Jim = J   David = J + 3   Tom = J - 5

Figure 7–3 *Student work for the How Old? problem*

About the Math

In this problem, students were challenged to use logic and reasoning to solve for the unknown quantities (the ages of all three boys) in addition to number and operation skills to verify their answers. They used the NCTM (2000) algebra content standards of representing the idea of a variable as an unknown quantity, using a letter or symbol and expressing mathematical relationships using equations. This was a multi-step problem that required them first to solve for unknowns, then check that their solutions were valid, and then apply what they knew to determine new information.

In solving this problem, students were required to use their knowledge of operations, of equations, and of logic and reasoning to arrive at a solution that made sense. This problem was not easy for any of the students, yet nearly all of them were able to work through their processing with the use of representations and arrive at a common solution.

Geometry

Geometry is a significant branch of mathematics, the one most visible in the physical world. (Burns 2002, 79)

Children have a natural curiosity about geometry. From an early age, they manipulate shapes, observe how they are similar and different, see how they fit together, and use them to create designs. They enjoy pointing out familiar shapes in their environment and experimenting with combining shapes to create new shapes. It is our role to help develop students' spatial abilities, and we should use varied experiences to help students connect geometry to ideas in number, patterns, and measurement. Students in grades 6 through 8 are moving beyond merely sorting and classifying shapes according to a shape's properties. They also are manipulating shapes and exploring the concepts of motion, location, and orientation. "The study of geometry in grades 6–8 requires thinking *and* doing" (NCTM 2000, 165). By embedding these experiences in problem-solving activities, we encourage students to investigate patterns in shapes and to use reasoning skills in a spatial context.

The Problem Task

The next task was adapted from Marilyn Burns, *A Collection of Math Lessons* (1987), and was posed to a sixth-grade class. The purpose of this lesson was to observe the students' problem-solving skills and their ability to use information about the characteristics of a pentomino to find all possible combinations of pentominoes. This activity was presented to a group of students with no prior experience in using pentominoes.

Rather than give the students a task to complete, Mrs. Long began the lesson with a concept formation chart that showed an example of a pentomino and a nonexample. Because she didn't want to use the correct term for the shapes, she started by telling the group, "Today we are going to take a look at a mystery shape that has certain characteristics. All of the shapes in the set have the same unique characteristics." She asked the students to look at the shapes and see if they could define differences in them. Without asking for discussion, she put up one more shape in each column. Because the students now had four different shapes to compare, many of them began offering what they saw as similarities and differences in the examples. One student commented that they looked like dominoes put together, and another saw that the shapes in the example column all had five smaller squares. Mrs. Long asked them to look at the number of squares in the nonexamples so that they could determine if having five smaller squares was indeed one of the characteristics of this mystery shape. Before they could respond, she showed them the third set of examples and nonexamples. When the third set was shown, many of the students had a puzzled look on their face because the nonexample also had five smaller squares. (See Figure 7–4.)

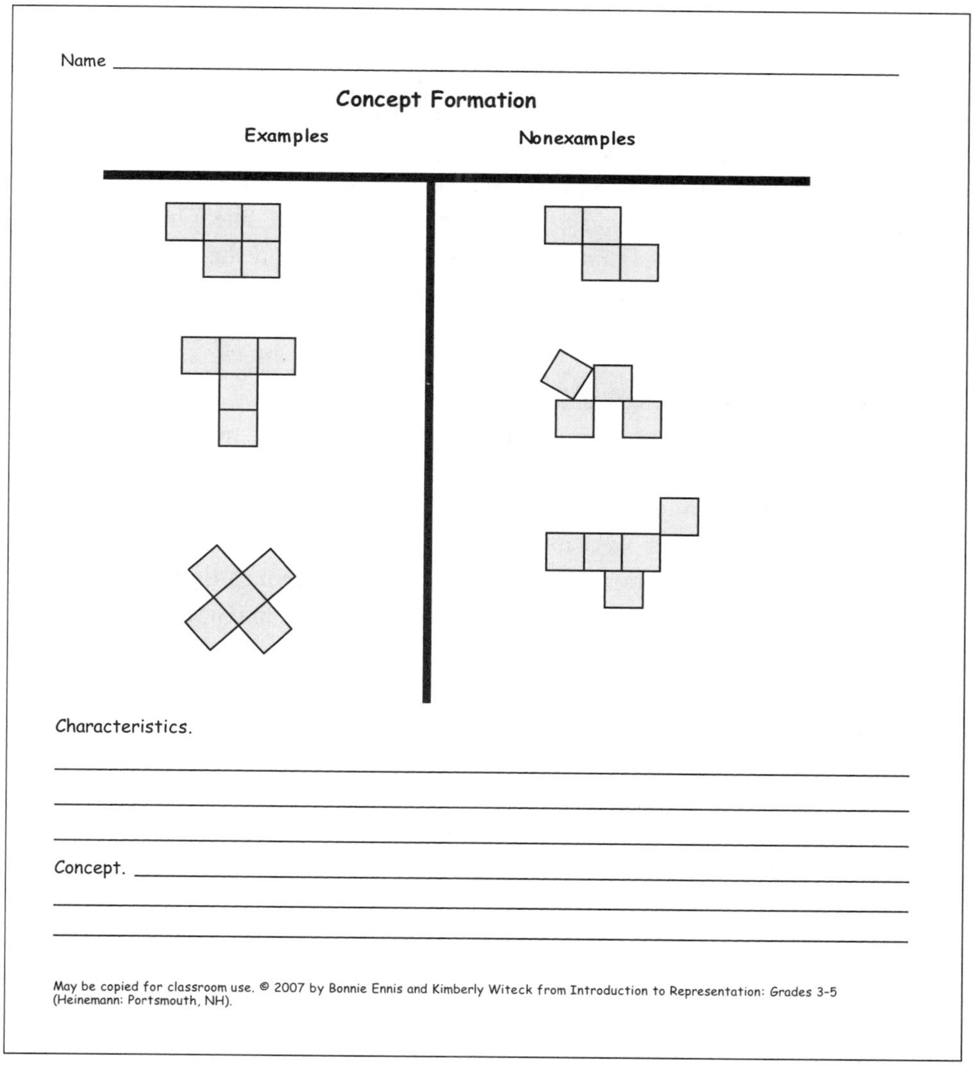
Name ______

Concept Formation

Examples | **Nonexamples**

Characteristics. ______

Concept. ______

May be copied for classroom use. © 2007 by Bonnie Ennis and Kimberly Witeck from Introduction to Representation: Grades 3-5 (Heinemann: Portsmouth, NH).

Figure 7–4 *Concept formation chart for pentominoes*

At this point, Mrs. Long asked students to use their tiles to create the examples and nonexamples at their tables. By having the students re-create the shapes, her hope was that they would begin to see the differences and similarities even though the number of examples was limited. After a few minutes, she again asked them if they could define the characteristics of the mystery shape given what they now know. One student offered that they still thought that characteristic of having five squares was important in this figure even though one of the shapes in the nonexamples also had five squares. Another student stated that it seemed like the examples were "neater." Mrs. Long asked what he meant by neater? The student replied, "It just looks like they are straighter and lined up neater in the examples. If you look at the nonexamples, two of them have a square that is connected at a corner and another square that is between two other squares."

The discussion continued for a little while longer until Mrs. Long asked the students to write at the bottom of their paper what they thought were the two main characteristics of the shape and to share their thoughts with others at their table. When everyone had finished doing this, Mrs. Long again asked for their thoughts. This time, instead of writing, she picked up a handful of tiles and said, "What do I need to do to have a shape that fits in with the rest of these?" Margaret said, "Take five tiles and put them under the document camera and slide the sides together." Mrs. Long followed Margaret's directions, but she deliberately slid two squares together so that they were not lined up evenly on one side. Margaret told her to move the squares so that the edges were even and one entire side was touching another complete side. Once Mrs. Long was finished, she had a shape that looked like the letter L, and she asked the class if everyone agreed with the example. With heads nodding, she was almost ready to give them work time to find all of the possible shapes, but at this point, she had not named the shape.

So as she redefined the characteristics, she talked about the name given to this shape. "What do you call a shape with five sides?" Everyone responded at once with the name "pentagon," so she continued to share with them that this shape begins with the same prefix and is called a *pentomino*.

She explained that there were exactly twelve pentominoes to be found. She had already given them four examples, and now she wanted them to find the rest of the examples, but before starting, she wanted them to understand that a shape reflected or rotated was not a different shape. Using the L pentomino as an example, she flipped it over and told them that just because it had a different orientation, it was not a different pentomino. Their task was to find the other eight shapes in the set. Students were instructed to arrange their tiles until they thought they had a different pentomino, and then they needed to draw the shape on their graph paper.

The students got to work, and Mrs. Long circulated around the room commenting when she saw a new pentomino. As the students were working, she would occasionally have students go to the front and draw their pentomino on the large graph paper she had on the board. When all twelve pentominoes had been drawn on the graph paper, she asked the students to look at them and see if they could name the shapes. Even though some of them did not look exactly like a letter of the alphabet, she wanted each of them associated with a letter. By doing this, it allows students to see if any pieces are missing in their set, and later on when they work with them again, she can call the pentomino by its name. Once the pentominoes were named, she gave each student an individual set and allowed for free exploration for the remaining time.

About the Math

The main objective of this lesson was to introduce the pentomino but in a manner that allowed students an opportunity to construct meaning about the shapes' characteristics. Using the concept formation chart, students had time to process the characteristics of a pentomino as opposed to remembering them. By challenging the students to discover the remaining eight pentominoes, they were constantly applying the characteristics to the new shapes they were creating. Later, these shapes will be used for a number of geometry topics. Pentominoes can be used to study and illustrate symmetry, congruence, area, and perimeter, among others. In addition, there are a number of commercially produced puzzles and activities designed for use with these shapes. The books *Chasing Vermeer* by Blue Balliett (2004) and its sequel, *The Wright 3* (2006), are both wonderful magical books that weave pentominoes into their mystery. Students will enjoy reading the books, especially after they have used the pentominoes in class.

Measurement

Measurement is a process that students in grades 3–5 use every day as they explore questions related to their school or home environment. (NCTM 2000, 171)

Measurement, like geometry, is an area about which students have a natural curiosity. Even very young children enjoy using tools such as rulers and measuring tapes to measure the length of objects, and they experiment with different concepts in measurement, such as time: "I'm coming to your house at fourteen o'clock!" As children get older, their understanding of what it means to measure an object grows, and in grades 6 through 8, students' understanding of the use of measurement should deepen and expand. Through many varied and hands-on activities, students begin to deepen their understanding of these concepts and learn to correctly recognize when a situation involves an area or perimeter formula or both. They begin to develop and use formulas to help them expand measurements to concepts of proportionality. They also begin to have more of an appreciation for units of volume and have clear benchmarks in their minds, such as a gallon jug, a two-liter soda bottle, and a pint of milk. It is important for teachers at this stage to help students connect ideas within measurement with other mathematical concepts and other disciplines, such as art and music.

The Problem Task

A rectangular sheet of wood has four small squares removed. It is then cut to make a box that is 5 cm by 4 cm with a volume of 60 cm³. (Four pieces the size of A4 are removed.)

Find the original area of the sheet of wood. (See Figure 7–5.)

This task was given to a group of seventh-grade prealgebra students. The purpose of the task was to provide students with an opportunity to apply already learned information about finding the area of a rectangle to a new formula (volume) to determine the total area measurement. To complete the task, the students had access to square tiles, rulers, centimeter graph paper, tape, construction paper, and pencils. Mrs. Williams directed them to complete the task in pairs but said they could ask for assistance from other students in the class or clarification from her if they wanted.

Before starting, a few students raised their hand to say that they thought there was information missing from the problem. They didn't think it could be answered because they didn't have all of the information needed to find the area of the original rectangle. Mrs. Williams told them to go back and look at the drawing and the measurements given because they had everything needed to solve the problem. She also told them that they could look in a math dictionary for the procedure for finding volume if they thought it would provide useful information.

Ryan and Kurt's group started drawing the shape on their centimeter graph paper. Ryan still was not sure if they had all of the information, and he and Kurt questioned how they could complete the diagram if so many measurements were missing. Finally, Kurt said, "Let's just guess about the measurements we don't know, and maybe when we finish the box, we will be able to figure out how high the sides are going to be." They finished their drawing, cut the shape out around the edges, and taped the sides together to form a box. As they looked around the room, several students had also begun putting their box together. Ryan asked one of the groups how high they measured the sides of the box. Everyone seemed to have just guessed on that measure. Mrs. Williams stopped by another desk and overheard Mike and Jerry talking about their box. It seemed as if they were closest to seeing the relationship between the formula for volume and the missing measure. Mike even wrote the formula on the bottom of the

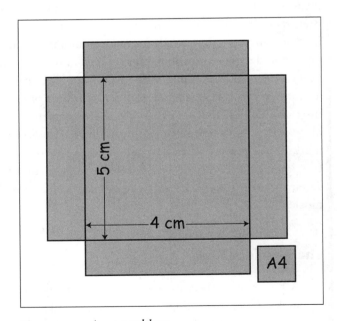

Figure 7–5 *Area problem*

box they made and began substituting the values in for the missing pieces. Because they still didn't have the height measure, the equation they wrote was $4 \times 5 \times h = 60$. When they went back to the math dictionary and saw the definition of the formula for the volume of a rectangular prism, they begin to think that maybe they needed to use centimeter cubes to see the height of the box.

After some discussion, they decided that they could solve the equation since only one variable was missing. Their solution to the equation was $4 \times 5 \times h = 60$, $20h = 60$, $h = 3$. With the answer that the height was 3, they now went back to their problem and determined that since the A4 sections were called squares, they must have four equal sides, and those sides must measure 3 centimeters each. Determined to be the first to finish, they started drawing another rectangle that had the missing measures. Since all of the sides had two squares missing, they said that you have to add 6 centimeters to each measurement, giving you a rectangle that measure 11 cm by 10 cm, which meant the area of the original sheet of wood must be 110 cm^3.

Since most of the other groups were finishing up, Mrs. Williams asked Mike and Jerry to take their work to the front and explain how they determined their answer.

About the Math

This multi-step task required students to draw on their understanding of what area is, their spatial awareness, and their developing understanding of volume.

Students also used problem-solving skills to complete the task. If their initial approach proved unsuccessful, they were encouraged to think about how they could modify their work. In this case, modifying meant looking to see how they could find the missing measure instead of giving up on the problem. They were also challenged to create a three-dimensional representation of their two-dimensional shape, a skill that is not easy for some students but that must be developed. Representation in the forms of tiles and drawings proved essential to completing this task successfully. In addition, students not only had to find a single answer, but they also needed to apply that answer in finding the solution to the problem.

Data Analysis: Statistics and Probability

Learning to interpret, use, and construct useful representations needs careful and deliberate attention in the classroom. (NCTM 2000)

The purpose of data analysis is to answer an engaging question, a question that has real implications, and one that can be answered by collecting, organizing, displaying, and interpreting data. Students in grades 6 through 8 should have multiple opportunities to interpret data and decide which data display to use. Only by using a variety of data displays that are both real and meaningful will students understand the factors involved in making those decisions. Because the very act of collecting data is the direct result of asking a question, that question occasionally leads to a prediction about the data results, which can take place prior to the data collection but also after the data have been collected and analyzed. Before collecting data, the teacher might ask, "What do you think the data will show?" Or once the data have been collected, he could ask, "What do you think will happen next?" It is because of this close relationship that the terms *statistics* and *probability* are usually encompassed through the term *data analysis*.

Nothing can excite a group of middle grades math students more than seeing food and technology as part of their lesson. As students entered Mrs. Sullivan's eighth-grade math classroom, they were excited to see tubs of tiny fish crackers. Each group of students would have a clear tub that had been filled with one variety of the crackers. (See Figure 7–6.) In addition to the tubs of crackers, each group would have another smaller container of colorful fish crackers, a small aquarium net, a plastic tray, and a folder of recording sheets.

As an opening activity and to focus the students on what was about to happen, Mrs. Sullivan had set up a slide show of pictures showing a variety of wildlife. Whales, bears, birds, and insects in their natural habitat were scrolling across her white board. As the slide show ended, a video clip started that showed a group of dolphin watchers counting dolphins in the surf.

Once the clip had finished, Mrs. Sullivan asked the students to talk about what they had seen on the clip and the slide show. A few of them commented on how nice the pictures were and how important it was to protect animal habitats. Sam wanted to know if they were going to get to eat the crackers. Mrs. Sullivan assured him that he would get to eat some of them, but first, she wanted to use them to practice what bi-

Figure 7–6 *Tub of fish crackers*

ologist sometimes call *capture and count* or *capture and recapture*. She continued to tell them that it was important to assess the health of bodies of water, and one way to accomplish this is to make sure the fish population is continuing to flourish. Using one of the tubs as an example, she began talking about the process of determining the number of fish in a body of water. She said, "Suppose scientist are becoming concerned that this lake is not as healthy as it should be, and it is necessary to determine if the population of fish has decreased over the years."

She asked the students to think about how a marine biologist could go about determining the number of fish in a lake or pond. Comments such as using divers to go down and count or getting boats with clear bottoms so you could see under the water were offered. Sam said you could get a bunch of fisherman to catch fish all today and keep track of them. Since students were obviously not familiar with the capture and count method of estimating populations, she explained the process to them. She said, "In this procedure, biologists will catch a quantity of fish, count them, tag them, and release them back into the body of water. After a few days, to allow them to mix back in with the rest of the population, they begin catching the fish again." She proceeded to tell them that since the scientist knew how many tagged fish they had; they could use that number to determine an estimate of the entire lake's population.

At this point, she took a package of colorful fish crackers and said, "I know I have 225 fish in this container, so these fish will represent my tagged fish. I can tell them apart from the rest of the fish because of their color." She then dumped the fish into her lake. She asked the students if they could come up with the ratio of tagged fish to total fish. Ann came to the board and wrote the ratio 225 / x, with x being the unknown number of total fish. The students were asked to talk in their groups about how this information could be useful. After some conversation, one student offered his solution of catching the fish using the net and counting how many tagged fish were in the sample. This information, he continued, could be used to set up a proportion that could be solved for x.

Now that the students had an idea of what needed to happen, she asked them how many samples they thought they should collect. "About one hundred," one student said. "How do we know when we have enough?" Mrs. Sullivan asked. The point she was trying to make is that there is no magical number for samples, but one or two samples is not enough on which to base a prediction. She asked the students to take the recording sheets from their folders and look at the information each group was being asked to collect. The first step was to count their "tagged' fish for release into their lake. They then needed to use their net to mix up the populations before beginning the sampling. Each sample would consist of one catch, and they would need to count the number of tagged fish and total fish in the sample and record the information on their sheet.

Once counted, the fish needed to be returned to the lake and mixed in with the rest before another catch occurred. She asked each group to simplify their samples, record them as one ratio on the spreadsheet, and graph their results. She had already created a spreadsheet with the formulas needed to simplify the ratios so that all of the group's samples would be combined into one ratio for comparison to the population, and she would use the graphing function of the program to finalize a class graph. At this point, all of the groups began their sampling, and true to her word, Mrs. Sullivan brought each group an individual package of crackers to eat as they fished.

As groups recorded their findings, the results were displayed on the projector for each of the groups to see. The final proportion needing to be solved was:

$$\frac{4 \text{ tagged fish in sample}}{24 \text{ fish in sample}} = \frac{225 \text{ total tagged}}{x \text{ in lake}}$$

Solving the proportion, the class determined that the lake had a total of 1,350 fish. Additional discussions centered on the data that individual groups had and the comparison to the final results.

The Role of the Teacher

Simulations are important because they give students a sense for how the mathematics they are learning in class connects with real-world experiences. In this case, students had an opportunity to replicate a real-world procedure and analyze data that they collected. They not only collected the data, but they also graphed the information so that they had a visual picture of the information they found. Representations are useful tools for supporting children's learning across all the mathematical strands. By learning how to show their thinking, students are developing skills that will serve them well as they progress into more advanced mathematics. We should support this growth by providing students with many opportunities to experience math in a tactile as well as visual way and by helping them to communicate their thinking through the use of manipulatives, pictures and diagrams, graphs, and numbers and symbols.

Questions for Discussion

1. In what ways can we connect the NCTM Content Standards with the Process Standards?

2. How could using tiles help students solve the first problem in this chapter, The Cookie Caper?

3. Some teachers argue that using manipulatives slows down the instructional process. What arguments can you give to help change their thoughts?

4. What other simulations could be used to help students see how the math done in their classroom has real-world implications?

Accepting the Challenge

The Representation Standard

Principles and Standards for School Mathematics (NCTM 2000) describes representations as fundamental to understanding and applying mathematics. Representations give students a vehicle through which to process their thoughts, a mechanism to organize information, and an avenue for communicating about mathematics. The ways students use them give us, their teachers, insight into their level of understanding about various mathematical concepts, and they provide us with visual, hands-on ways to teach mathematics. In this book, we have discussed the importance of helping students learn to represent their mathematical thinking and ways they can do so. The very act of creating a representation of a concept helps to form an image of that knowledge in a student's mind and therefore a deeper understanding of that concept (Marzano et al. 2001). The goal of this book is to define what representations are, discuss the value in using them to explore mathematical topics, and illustrate how they might be used in a mathematics classroom. Through student work samples, examples of different representations, and activity suggestions, we hope to have made the case that the use of representations should be an integral component of any mathematics program.

Representations Support Learning

When students are learning to read, their teachers help them to develop a wide variety of strategies that will enable them to become confident, competent readers. Why should math be any different? Representation in math supports learning and helps students to develop a repertoire of strategies from which to pull when faced with novel tasks. For example, students who know how to use blocks to represent equal groups, a repeating pattern, or the value of a number have models in their minds that they can reconstruct or simply visualize when attempting to solve a new or challenging problem. Students who are able to take a set of data and not only organize it into a chart or graph but also interpret it in a way to make meaning of it have skills that they can use when faced with new or large amounts of information. Students who can generate a picture to show their understanding of a problem and then use the picture to help them solve the problem own a strategy that they can choose to use in many different situations. In addition, students who can apply numbers and symbols in a meaningful way to simple or complex mathematical processes are making connections between the concrete and abstract. Representations really support and show evidence of learning!

Manipulatives in Different Forms

Manipulatives come in many different forms, both concrete and virtual, and provide students and teachers with a means to model different mathematical concepts and processes. How can we expect students to understand the value of numbers if they are exposed to the numbers only in digit form? It is through building and manipulating concrete numeric representations that students begin to get a sense of how small and large numbers really can be and what the digits in a number stand for. Using fraction circles or squares gives students a visual, concrete means to explore concepts such as one whole and one-half in addition to equivalent and nonequivalent fractions. How can we expect students to draw a representation of a fraction if they have not seen a perfectly proportioned one as they would with fraction tiles? Manipulatives provide us with concrete, visual benchmarks of certain mathematical concepts on which we can draw later.

Virtual manipulatives offer students and teachers additional experiences in representing mathematical concepts. There isn't the threat of running out of blocks, and students can print an instant paper copy of their representation. In addition, while some older students might find it juvenile to use blocks, tiles, and other concrete manipulatives, they are excited about manipulating images of those blocks on the computer. An interactive white board provides a means for students to show their approach to solving a problem so that all their peers can see, which helps facilitate group discussion and strategizing. Technology is opening up a new world of possibilities for both teachers and students for exploring mathematical concepts.

We need to devote some time to thinking about which manipulatives we choose to use with our students, as different manipulatives can result in students constructing different understandings. Students whose early math experiences are with base ten blocks, for example, are more likely to develop a units view of numbers (such as hundreds, tens, and ones), whereas students who have many experiences with tools associated with counting, such as hundreds boards or number lines, are more likely to see the counting aspects associated with solving certain problems. Models used to represent middle grades algebra concepts need to be introduced carefully. Students need to understand and recognize the relative size of the manipulative as it relates to the actual unit. As an example, some manipulatives are proportional, making the comparison of units part of the process; however, there are manipulatives that may appear to have a proportional relationship among the pieces but in fact are not. Careful consideration about the influence manipulatives may have on students' understandings is a necessary part of the planning process.

Pictures and Diagrams

Pictures and diagrams are useful tools for young mathematicians as they attempt to create meaning from mathematical situations. They are a natural next step after manipulatives as students progress from the concrete to the abstract. As students deal with more and more complex concepts and larger numbers, they may find it necessary to rely on alternative representations, such as pictures and diagrams, because concrete manipulatives may become too cumbersome. It is important to stress, however, that this progression from the concrete to the abstract should occur when a student has a deep understanding of a mathematical concept and can communicate that understanding through concrete representations and words.

Pictures can give us great insight into a student's level of understanding about a concept. The ability to take the words from a math story or the numbers of a computation problem and create a visual representation in the form of a picture requires an understanding of the problem at hand. We can use the information we gain from studying students' pictorial representations to make instructional decisions that will meet their needs. Similarly, students can use the pictures or diagrams they create to help them communicate their thinking to others. It is often much easier for students to talk about a picture they have created to process a problem than it is to explain in words alone how they solved it. Working with our students to become proficient and efficient in creating pictorial representations should be one of our goals as we help to develop our students' mathematical abilities.

Diagrams, like pictures, provide students with another way to show understanding. Venn diagrams are extremely useful in helping organize students' thoughts about similarities and differences between two or more objects or concepts. We must be sure to include activities with graphic organizers such as Venn diagrams, flowcharts, and T-charts to help students develop these comparison skills. The ability to compare and contrast requires high-level thinking at the analytical level, which leads to deeper understandings.

Numbers and Symbols

Just as students progress from concrete manipulatives to pictorial representations, they then progress to perhaps the most abstract form of representation: numbers and symbols. As students mature in their mathematical understandings, they reach a point where they are ready to learn about the numbers and symbols associated with concepts and processes. Timing is very important: To introduce the abstract too early may result in shutting down the meaning- and sense-making processes in students, and they may become overly concerned with memorizing procedures and formulas rather than thinking about the mathematics involved in a situation. An important role of the teacher is to be attuned to each student's level of understanding at the concrete level *before* attempting to introduce numbers or symbols.

Once students have demonstrated a deep understanding of a mathematical concept, we have to be sure that they then develop a deep understanding of the numbers and symbols they will be using. It is absolutely essential that there is no confusion about what the equal sign means. We need to assess our students' understanding of this very basic and important element of an equation and clear up any misunderstandings that may exist. Without this fundamental knowledge, equations have little meaning to students, and as they progress in higher-level mathematics, the holes in their understandings will grow.

Invented algorithms are wonderful windows into a student's mind. Their unique ways of interpreting a problem and applying their own understandings to its solution provide us with a good idea of what their level of understanding is and if there are any misconceptions. The invented procedures can also show us how students think about numbers. For example, if, when faced with a multidigit multiplication problem, a student breaks up the numbers into units, finds partial products, and then combines the parts to get a total, we can feel somewhat confident that the student has an understanding of place value and what the different steps in such a problem really mean. Information like this is invaluable as we plan experiences that will challenge our students and will also allow them to draw on their current understandings about different concepts.

Tables and Graphs

The purpose of graphing is to organize data in a meaningful display to make analysis of data easier. With this in mind, we need to plan meaningful experiences with graphing for our students. It is not enough to simply hand them a set of numbers and ask them to create a bar graph. Little understanding is developed through this passive approach to working with data. Rather, we need to think about graphing data with a purpose in mind: to answer a question that we or our students have posed and about which data have been collected. Then, after the data have been displayed on the appropriate type of graph, we must use it to answer the question originally posed.

Many of us spend too much time on ensuring that our students know how to label a graph correctly and not enough time on helping students think about which graph would be most appropriate to display a set of data. Students need many experiences with different types of graphs so that they become familiar with their purposes and can make appropriate choices about which graph would be best for the task at hand. For example, students who choose to display the number of shoppers at a mall over an eight-hour period on a bar graph are not showing a deep understanding of the purpose of a bar graph or of the data. A line graph would be more appropriate for this type of data, and unless we give students many experiences creating and analyzing line graphs, they will probably be unable to correctly assign a line graph to a certain situation.

In addition to bar and line graphs, students in grades 6 through 8 should become proficient with line plots, circle graphs, double-line graphs, double-bar graphs, stem-and-leaf plots, and box-and-whisker plots. They need to do more than just see them and hear about them; they need to create them using meaningful data and analyze them. Bulletin boards are wonderful ways to display large graphs of different types. They are visible to the whole class, and they can be analyzed by the whole group, small groups, or individuals. In the five minutes before lunch or dismissal, you can ask students to generate some true statements about the data on the graph. Two different graphs displayed side by side can serve as an opportunity to compare and contrast the two methods of displaying data and can serve as a discussion point about why each graph was chosen for the data it represents. Large visuals such as these can also allow for whole-group discussion about the shape of the data and about generalizations that can be made regarding the information displayed.

Graphing data is a wonderful tool for cross-curricular and multicultural activities and should be an integral part of our students' learning. With the vast resources available to us such as the Internet, newspapers, textbooks, and people around us, students should have many opportunities to think about topics that interest them and then be able to research those topics to collect data and organize the data in an appropriate display. This active engagement in data analysis will help our students develop their critical and analytical skills with tasks that have meaning and are of interest to them.

Assessing Students' Representations

One of the more challenging aspects of a teacher's work is assessing student progress. Traditionally, the purpose of assessing students was to give teachers data to assign a grade. Fortunately, we use assessments for more meaningful purposes now, although we often still attach a grade to student performance. Assessment takes many forms, both formal and informal, and can be used to inform instruction, help students think about their learning, help parents understand their child's progress, and most important, give us information about a student's level of understanding.

When faced with the task of assessing students' representations, we need to consider our purpose for assessing. Is it to get a quick idea of whether or not a student understands a concept? Are we looking for mastery of a concept or skill? Are we looking for developmental growth in their use of representations? Depending on the desired outcome of the assessment, we have several different options. We might simply listen in to a conversation between two students as they work together to solve a problem, making anecdotal notes as necessary. Or we might assign a performance-based assessment, asking students to represent a concept in a way that makes sense to them. We might also assign a task and collect paper copies of the representations the students did, analyzing them at a later time, perhaps using a rubric. Or we may just ask a student to explain what he or she is thinking about a particular problem. Each of these forms of assessment can help us as we plan meaningful mathematical experiences for our students.

How Classroom Teachers Can Make This Work

As teachers, we often have the most control over our students' immediate learning environment. We spend much time planning the layout of the room, the correct seating arrangement to ensure collaborative work, and the right displays for the walls to help the room seem inviting and comfortable for our students. In most classrooms, there is a library that is visible and accessible to the students, but are there math tools in a visible and accessible location? Do we have number lines, graphics, and other mathematical representations hanging in our room to help support our students' learning in math as we do in language arts? A wonderful compliment for us to receive as teachers is that we have as much numeracy visible in our room as we do literacy. We must strive to balance our efforts in all areas of the curriculum and to include as many mathematical displays as we do reading displays.

Having math tools in a visible and accessible location sends the message to our students and others that math is important and that we will use whatever tools are necessary to help us develop our mathematical thinking. Baskets of base ten blocks, counters, pattern blocks, algebra tiles, cubes, dice, rulers, string, markers, grid paper, and calculators, just to name a few, are some of the tools we want to provide our students the opportunity to use. Because math manipulatives can get expensive, one way to build up our classroom supply is to solicit some from our students' parents and our colleagues. There are many items in our homes that can serve as math manipulatives, such as coins, beans, toothpicks, craft sticks, ribbon, and containers, and parents are usually more than happy to help out by sending them in. We just have to ask.

One of the most important ways we can help to develop our students into competent and confident mathematicians is to become competent and confident mathematicians ourselves. It is not enough to rely on the math we learned in elementary school. A quick survey of our colleagues will likely show that the way they learned math was not a process of concept development and understanding but rather a process of memorizing algorithms and procedures and doing as they were told. Fortunately, that approach to mathematics instruction is no longer the norm. However, it places a new challenge on us to go back and develop a deep understanding of the mathematical concepts we experienced only superficially when we were in school. Community colleges, local universities, and district-provided professional development offer ways we can relearn the math that we will be teaching our students. Without this strong content knowledge, it is difficult to analyze our students' representations to determine their level of understanding about a concept and then to determine the next steps to further their growth. It is only through having a deep understanding of the mathematics ourselves that we will be able to anticipate misconceptions by our students and to push our students to think more deeply about mathematics.

How School Administrators Can Make This Work

Classroom teachers have the most direct impact on students' learning, but there are many ways school administrators can help to support them in this task. First, they can allocate funds to purchase high-quality math materials, such as base ten blocks, pattern blocks, geometric solids, fraction circles or squares, tiles, geoboards, and Cuisenaire rods, as well as invest in technology that will support student representations, such as software and interactive white boards. Although it would be wonderful to have a class set of manipulatives in each room, at the minimum there should be one set for every two classrooms to share.

Second, administrators can work with teachers and specialists to set up the master schedule so that team members have time to collaborate and talk about the mathematics they are teaching and to actually experience concepts and activities *before* introducing them to students. This is one of the best means for anticipating student misconceptions and planning appropriate responses to them.

Finally, administrators can support professional development that will enhance their teachers' math content knowledge. This can be done by paying for teachers to attend math content classes, inviting a math consultant to come to the school, and purchasing teacher resources such as books and materials. School administrators are the instructional leaders in the school. By modeling a learning spirit, they encourage their teachers to further develop themselves.

Another way administrators can help students deepen their mathematical understandings through representations is by displaying representations around the school. With the help of the student council association, they can conduct a survey of students to learn about their suggestions for spirit days throughout the year. The data can be compiled into a graphic display and posted in the main hall (or outside the gymnasium, where there always seems to be some downtime!) or other central location where students will be able to see it, think about it, and discuss it. Another suggestion is to work with the school librarian to display information about types of books checked out by grade level. Again, student representatives could help in creating the data display. Aside from graphic representations, administrators can support the display of visual representations around the school by encouraging classroom teachers to hang outside their rooms student-generated examples from completed class activities, such as Venn diagrams or representations of sorted polygons. By communicating the message through words and actions that mathematical learning is important and valued, administrators can support teacher efforts to develop competent, confident mathematicians.

The Challenge to Teachers

We are entering a new and exciting era of teaching and learning mathematics, one that challenges students to explore, struggle with, and create their own understandings of mathematical concepts. Students are no longer handed knowledge through formulas or algorithms but instead develop their own knowledge as a result of first-hand experiences. To meet this challenge, we must be willing to rethink the way we approach mathematics instruction. We must begin to view ourselves as experts in the content we teach, and as such, we need to do whatever it takes to become an expert: take a math content course, engage in regular dialogue with our colleagues about the math we teach, attend professional development seminars, and so on. To help our students think deeply about the mathematics they are learning, we must also think deeply about it.

The use of representations provides a particularly exciting opportunity to begin to think in more depth about math content. How will we use manipulatives to get children to think about the magnitude of a number? How will we show in pictorial form the meaning of a math story? In what ways can we use numbers and symbols to synthesize our thinking? These are questions we must ask of ourselves at the same time that we are asking our students to represent their thinking. It is a wonderful, exciting time to be a math teacher, and to meet the challenge of preparing our students to become confident, competent mathematicians, we must also become the same.

Questions for Discussion

1. What are the most important pieces of knowledge you have gained from reading this book?

2. What are ways teachers can support an environment that values mathematical representations?

3. What are ways administrators can support an environment that values mathematical representations?

4. How will you change aspects of your instructional planning to ensure that you give deep thought to the mathematics before introducing it to students?

The following resources are meant to support you as you continue to explore the representation standard in grades 6 through 8. You will find a variety of text resources—books that will provide you with additional activities and instructional strategies that will encourage student representations. A list of math-related literature books and math websites is included to supply you with classroom tasks, electronic manipulative ideas, and teacher resources.

Text Resources

The following text resources provide a variety of activities and strategies for supporting students as they develop their skills in representing mathematical thinking.

Andrini, B. 1991. *Cooperative Learning and Mathematics*. San Juan Capistrano, CA: Resources for Teachers.

Balka, D., and L. Boswell. 2006. *Working with Algebra Tiles*. Rowley, MA: Didax.

Barnett, C., D. Goldenstein, and B. Jackson, 1994. *Fractions, Decimals, Ratios, and Percents: Hard to Teach and Hard to Learn*. Portsmouth, NH: Heinemann.

Bender, W. 2005. *Differentiating Math Instruction: Strategies That Work for K–8 Classrooms*. Thousand Oaks, CA: Sage.

Bosse, N. R. 1995. *Writing Mathematics*. Chicago: Creative.

Burns, M. 1992. *The Way to Math Solutions*. Sausalito, CA: Math Solutions.

———. 2002. *About Teaching Mathematics*. Sausalito, CA: Math Solutions.

Burns, M., and C. Humphreys, 1990, *A Collection of Math Lessons, 6–8*. Sausalito, CA: Math Solutions.

Burns, M., B. Tank, and T. Stone. 1987. *A Collection of Math Lessons, 3–6*. Sausalito, CA: Math Solutions.

Countryman, J. 1992. *Writing to Learn Mathematics*. Portsmouth, NH: Heinemann.

Kagan, S. 1992. *Cooperative Learning*. San Clemente, CA: Resources for Teachers.

McIntosh, M., and R. J. Draper. 1997. *Write Starts*. New York: Dale Seymour.

Miller, E. 2001. *Read It! Draw It! Solve It!* Parsippany, NJ: Dale Seymour.

Newman, V. 1994. *Math Journals*. San Diego: Teaching Resource Center.

O'Connell, S. 2001. *Math—The Write Way for Grades 2–3*. Columbus, OH: Frank Schaffer.

———. 2001. *Math—The Write Way for Grades 4–5*. Columbus, OH: Frank Schaffer.

———. 2005. *Now I Get It: Strategies for Building Confident and Competent Mathematicians K–6*. Portsmouth, NH: Heinemann.

Stewart, K., K. Walker, and C. Reak. 1995. *Thinking Questions for Pattern Blocks, Grades 1–3*. Chicago: Creative.

Van de Walle, J. A., and L. H. Lovin. 2005. *Teaching Student-Centered Mathematics, Grades 5–8*. New York: Pearson.

Wheatley, G., and G. Abshire. 2007. *Developing Mathematical Fluency, Activities for Grades 5–8*. Bethany Beach, DE: Mathematics Learning.

Whitin, P., and D. Whitin. 2000. *Math Is Language Too: Talking and Writing in the Mathematics Classroom*. Urbana, IL: National Council of Teachers of English.

———. 2003. *A Mathematical Passage: Strategies for Promoting Inquiry in Grades 4–6*. Portsmouth, NH: Heinemann.

Zikes, D. 2003. *Big Book of Math K–6*. San Antonio, TX: Dinah-Might Adventures.

Math-Literature Connections

One of the ways teachers can help students learn how to represent their mathematical thinking is by using literature books to anchor an activity or lesson. There are an increasing number of books on the market today designed to link math and reading.

Adler, D. 1998. *Shape Up! Fun with Triangles and Other Polygons*. New York: Holiday House.

Balliett, B. 2005. *Chasing Vermeer*. New York: Scholastic.

———. 2006. *The Wright 3*. New York: Scholastic.

Burns, M. 1994. *The Greedy Triangle*. New York: Scholastic.

———. 1997. *Spaghetti and Meatballs for All! A Mathematical Story*. New York: Scholastic.

Dahl, R. 1982. *The BFG*. New York: Puffin.

Lasky, K. 1994. *The Librarian Who Measured the Earth*. Boston: Little, Brown.

Neuschwander, C. 1997. *Sir Cumference and the First Round Table: A Math Adventure*. Watertown, MA: Charlesbridge.

———. 1999. *Sir Cumference and the Dragon of Pi: A Math Adventure*. Watertown, MA: Charlesbridge.

———. 2001 *Sir Cumference and the Great Knight of Angleland: A Math Adventure*. Watertown, MA: Charlesbridge.

———. 2003. *Sir Cumference and the Sword in the Cone: A Math Adventure*. Watertown, MA: Charlesbridge.

———. 2006. *Sir Cumference and the Isle of Immeter: A Math Adventure*. Watertown, MA: Charlesbridge.

Schlein, M. 1996. *More Than One*. New York: Greenwillow.

Schwartz, D. 1997. *How Much Is a Million?* New York: Mulberry.

———. 1999. *On Beyond a Million*. New York: Doubleday.

Scieszka, J., and L. Smith. 1995. *Math Curse*. New York: Viking.

Silverstein, S. 1974. *Where the Sidewalk Ends*. New York: HarperCollins.

Websites

The following websites provide ideas and activities to use with students in helping them represent their math thinking.

Egyptian Fractions

www.ics.uci.edu/~eppstein/numth/egypt/—This site, by Dr. David Eppstein of the University of California at Irvine, gives a summary of how Egyptian fractions were used and some examples of unit fraction sums.

www.mcs.surrey.ac.uk/Personal/R.Knott/Fractions/egyptian.html—Rob Knott's teacher-friendly webpage on Egyptian fractions with links to other sites on similar topics.

www.mathcats.com/explore/oldegyptianfractions.html—This kid-friendly website, called Math Cats, has a section on Egyptian fractions.

www.maa.org/editorial/mathgames/mathgames_07_19_04.html—The Mathematical Association of America's website on Egyptian fractions.

regentsprep.org/Regents/mathb/2B2/algfracteacher.htm—The Oswego City School District's page on Egyptian fractions.

Graphing

regentsprep.org/Regents/Math/data/stemleaf.htm—This is a short tutorial on stem-and-leaf plots from the Oswego City School District.

www.purplemath.com/modules/stemleaf.htm—From Purplemath, this site shows some of the connections between stem-and-leaf plots and histograms.

www.mathsrevision.net/gcse/pages.php?page=10—Provides examples of stem-and-leaf plots and other statistical models.

Rubrics

There are several great websites for making rubrics or using ready-made rubrics.

rubistar.4teachers.org/index.php
www.teach-nology.com/web_tools/rubrics/
www.teachervision.fen.com/teaching-methods/rubrics/4521.html
www.education-world.com/a_curr/curr248.shtml

Other Resources

www.nctm.org—The National Council of Teachers of Mathematics website.

Balliett, B. 2005. *Chasing Vermeer*. New York: Scholastic.

———. 2006. *The Wright 3*. New York: Scholastic.

Barnett, C., D. Goldenstein, and B. Jackson, 1994. *Fractions, Decimals, Ratios, and Percents: Hard to Teach and Hard to Learn*. Portsmouth, NH: Heinemann.

Burns, M. 1987. *A Collection of Math Lessons, from Grades 3 through 6*. Sausalito, CA: Math Solutions.

———. 2002. *About Teaching Mathematics*. Sausalito, CA: Math Solutions.

Chapin, S., C. O'Connor, and N. Anderson. *Classroom Discussions: Using Math Talk to Help Students Learn*. Sausalito, CA: Math Solutions.

Fisher, S., and C. Hartmann. 2005. "Math through the Mind's Eye." *Mathematics Teacher* 99 (4): 246–250.

Hiebert, J., T. Carpenter, E. Fennema, K. Fuson, D. Wearne, H. Murray, A. Oliver, and P. Human. 1997. *Making Sense*. Portsmouth, MH: Heinemann.

Hiebert, J., R. Gallimore, H. Garnier, K. Bogard Givvin, H. Hollingsworth, J. Jacobs, A. Miu-Ying Chui, D. Wearne, M. Smith, N. Kersting, A. Manaster, E. Tseng, W. Etterbeek, C. Manaster, P. Gonzales, and J. Stigler. 2003. *Teaching Mathematics in Seven Countries: Results from the TIMSS 1999 Video Study* (NCES 2003–013 Revised). Washington, DC: U.S. Department of Education, National Center for Education Statistics.

Marzano, R., D. Pickering, and J. Pollock. 2001. *Classroom Instruction That Works*. Alexandria, VA: Association for Supervision and Curriculum Development.

Moyer, P., J. Bolyard, and M. Spikell. 2002. "What Are Virtual Manipulatives?" *Teaching Children Mathematics*. Reston, VA: NCTM.

National Council of Teachers of Mathematics (NCTM). 1989. *Curriculum and Evaluation Standards for School Mathematics*. Reston, VA: NCTM.

———. 2000. *Principles and Standards for School Mathematics*. Reston, VA: NCTM.

———. 2002. *Assessment Standards for School Mathematics*. Reston, VA: NCTM

Neuschwander, C. 1997. *Sir Cumference and the First Round Table: A Math Adventure*. Watertown, MA: Charlesbridge.

Nolan, H. 2001. *How Much, How Many, How Far, How Heavy, How Long, How Tall Is 1,000?* Toronto: Kids Can Press.

Pallotta, J. 2003. *Count to a Million*. New York: Scholastic.

Schwartz, D. 1993. *How Much Is a Million?* New York: Mulberry Books.

Small, D., and M. Anderson. 2007. "Document Cameras Provide No Limit to Learning Math." *E School News*—http://hb1.eschoolnews.com/curriculum/?i=46417.

Why Are the Activities on a CD?

At first glance, the CD included with this book appears to be a collection of teaching tools and student activities, much like the activities that appear in many teacher resource books. But instead of taking a book to the copier to copy an activity, with the CD you can simply print the desired page on your home or work computer. No more standing in line at the copier or struggling to carefully position the book on the copier so you can make a clean copy. And with our busy schedules, we appreciate having activities that are classroom ready and aligned with our math standards.

You may want to simplify some tasks or add complexity to others. The problems on the CD often include several parts or have added challenge extensions. When it is appropriate for your students, simply delete these sections for a quick way to simplify or shorten the tasks.

Editing the CD to Motivate and Engage Students

Personalizing Tasks or Capitalizing on Students' Interests

The editable CD provides a quick and easy way to personalize math problems. Substituting students' names, the teacher's name, or a favorite restaurant, sports team, or location can immediately engage students.

You know the interests of your students. Mentioning their interests in your problems is a great way to increase their enthusiasm for the activities. Think about their favorite activities and simply substitute their interests for those that appear in the problems.

One teacher knew that many of her students were not interested in sports, so she decided to reword the following task to capture their interest. Note: This type of editing is also important when the problem situation may not be culturally appropriate for your students (e.g., your students don't play musical instruments or have 4-H clubs

127

in their area). Changing the type of sports played is another alternative to making the activity more meaningful for a particular group of students.

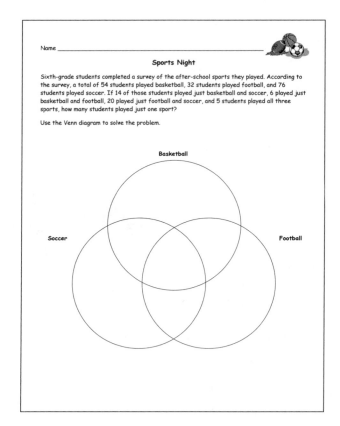

Name _____

Sports Night

Sixth-grade students completed a survey of the after-school sports they played. According to the survey, a total of 54 students played basketball, 32 students played football, and 76 students played soccer. If 14 of those students played just basketball and soccer, 6 played just basketball and football, 20 played just football and soccer, and 5 students played all three sports, how many students played just one sport?

Use the Venn diagram to solve the problem.

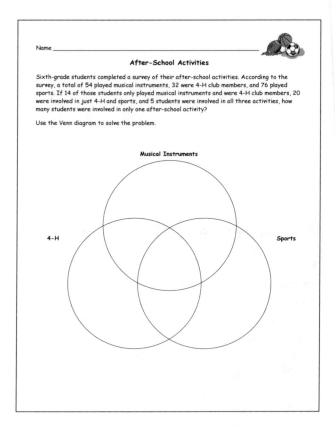

Name _____

After-School Activities

Sixth-grade students completed a survey of their after-school activities. According to the survey, a total of 54 played musical instruments, 32 were 4-H club members, and 76 played sports. If 14 of those students only played musical instruments and were 4-H club members, 20 were involved in just 4-H and sports, and 5 students were involved in all three activities, how many students were involved in only one after-school activity?

Use the Venn diagram to solve the problem.

Editing the CD to Differentiate Instruction

Creating Shortened or Tiered Tasks

While many students are able to move from one task to another, some students benefit from focusing on one task at a time. By simply separating parts of a task, either by cutting the page into sections or by using the editable CD feature to put the parts of the task on separate pages, teachers can help focus students on the first part of the task before moving them on to the next part.

In the next example, in which all the parts of the task initially appeared in one problem together, the different parts of the task are separated. Note that the spaces for student work and the lines for writing responses were widened for students who needed more space or larger lines for writing their responses. The first page of the example is shown. Each of the other five characters would have their own page.

Name _____

Cookie Caper

One night, the king went down into the royal kitchen where he found a basket full of cookies. He was hungry, so he ate $\frac{1}{6}$ of the cookies.

Show your work.

Explain your answer.

_____

_____

_____

_____

_____

Modifying the Readability of Tasks

Adding some fun details can generate interest and excitement in story problems, but you might prefer to modify some problems for students with limited reading ability. Simply deleting some of the words on the editable CD will result in an easy-to-read version of the same task, as shown in the second version of the following problem.

Name _____

What's Up Doc?

Farmer Fudd decided to grow a garden so he could make salad. He wants to make it 10.1 m long and 4.2 m wide. To prevent Big Bunny from entering his garden, he must make a fence surrounding the garden. He decides to make the fence 11.2 m long and 5.0 m wide. What is the area between the fence and the garden? Represent your solution with a diagram.

_____

Show the work for your solution.

Explain how you determined your answer.

_____

_____

_____

_____

_____

Name _____

What's Up Doc?

A farmer wants a garden 10.1 m long and 4.2 m wide.
He must make a fence around the garden that is 11.2 m long and 5.0 m wide.
What is the area between the fence and the garden?
Represent your solution with a diagram.

_____

Show your work.

Explain how you determined your answer.

_____

_____

_____

_____

_____

_____

Modifying Data

While all students may work on the same problem task, modifying the problem data will allow teachers to create varying versions of the task. Using the editable CD, you can either simplify the data or insert more challenging data, including larger numbers, fractions, decimals, or percentages. Changing the units of measure so that there are fewer conversions to calculate, as in the Orange Juice and Rope It Off problems, you can provide a way to differentiate the level of difficulty within a problem without changing the intent of the activity.

Name _____

Exit Tickets IV
Rope It Off

How many 9-inch pieces of rope can be cut from $1\frac{1}{2}$ yards of rope?

_____

Show your work.

Name _____

Orange Juice

Marita has $2\frac{1}{4}$ gallons of orange juice concentrate. It takes $\frac{3}{4}$ gallon to make a pitcher of orange juice. How many pitchers can she make?

_____

Show your work.

Name _____

Exit Tickets IV
Rope It Off

How many $7\frac{1}{4}$-inch pieces of rope can be cut from $1\frac{1}{2}$ yards of rope?

_____

Show your work.

Name _____

Orange Juice

Marita has $2\frac{1}{4}$ gallons of orange juice concentrate. It takes $\frac{3}{4}$ cups of the concentrate to make a pitcher of orange juice. How many pitchers can she make?

_____

Show your work.